Green Finance and Investment

Fossil-Fuel Subsidies in the EU's Eastern Partner Countries

ESTIMATES AND RECENT POLICY DEVELOPMENTS

OECD))

BETTER POLICIES FOR BETTER LIVES

This work is published under the responsibility of the Secretary-General of the OECD. The opinions expressed and arguments employed herein do not necessarily reflect the official views of OECD member countries.

This document, as well as any data and map included herein, are without prejudice to the status of or sovereignty over any territory, to the delimitation of international frontiers and boundaries and to the name of any territory, city or area.

Please cite this publication as:
OECD (2021), *Fossil-Fuel Subsidies in the EU's Eastern Partner Countries: Estimates and Recent Policy Developments*, Green Finance and Investment, OECD Publishing, Paris, *https://doi.org/10.1787/38d3a4b5-en*.

ISBN 978-92-64-71598-1 (print)
ISBN 978-92-64-42023-6 (pdf)

Green Finance and Investment
ISSN 2409-0336 (print)
ISSN 2409-0344 (online)

Foreword

This report summarises the main findings of the analysis of existing fossil-fuel subsidy schemes in the six European Union's Eastern Partner (EaP) countries – Armenia, Azerbaijan, Belarus, Georgia, Republic of Moldova and Ukraine. It briefly introduces the methodology used to identify and estimate government support for fossil-fuel production and consumption. It also discusses the main energy pricing and taxation policies that underline discussion on government support in the region's energy sector.

In 2018, to help governments in the EaP countries develop a better understanding of the economic, social and environmental impact of fossil-fuel subsidies, the Organisation for Economic Co-operation and Development (OECD) published the *Inventory of Energy Subsidies in the European Union's Eastern Partnership Countries*. As the first comprehensive assessment of this nature in the EaP region, the review analysed all types of energy subsidies provided over 2010-15. These included support to coal, oil (and petroleum products used particularly in the transport sector) and natural gas, as well as to renewable sources of energy and energy-efficiency measures.

This study updates the 2018 Inventory by providing data and estimates for 2016-19. It also briefly discusses the short-term COVID-19 related measures that the EaP governments put in place in 2020 to protect producers and consumers in the energy sector.

The analysis measures two major types of fossil-fuel subsidies: direct transfers of funds to producers and consumers; and tax expenditure and other foregone government revenue. The Annexes provide detailed estimates of all individual support measures for each of the countries.

The study relies on publicly available sources of information, such as public accounts, official documents related to subsidy monitoring and budget planning and reporting, academic literature and media items. It draws on these diverse sources to summarise the context, state of play and evolving landscape of fossil-fuel subsidies in the region. The **cut-off date for the data** and information used for analysis is **the end of 2019** unless otherwise indicated.

The study was prepared with the financial support of the European Union within the "European Union for Environment" (EU4Environment) Programme and of Germany's Federal Ministry for the Environment, Nature Conservation and Nuclear Safety, provided through its International Climate Initiative.

The views expressed herein are those of the authors only and can in no way be taken to reflect the official opinion of the European Union, its members, the Governments of the EaP countries or the EU4Environment implementing partners (OECD, United Nations Economic Commission for Europe, United Nations Environment Programme, United Nations Industrial Development Organization, and the World Bank).

The study was prepared within the framework of the GREEN Action Task Force hosted by the OECD Environment Directorate.

Acknowledgements

This report is a product of the collaborative efforts of many people and institutions, whose contributions are gratefully acknowledged.

Nelly Petkova (OECD, Environment Directorate) managed the project and contributed to the writing of the report. The report was drafted by Daniel Fjærtoft and Yuliia Oharenko (Sigra Group). A team of national experts collected the underlying data and information for the country-level analysis. The group of experts included: Tigran Sekoyan (Armenia), Ahmad Alili (Azerbaijan), Andrei Malochka (Belarus), Giorgi Mukhigulishvili (Georgia), Mihai Roscovan (Moldova) and Yuliia Oharenko (Ukraine).

A number of European Union's Eastern Partner (EaP) government officials and consultants provided valuable suggestions, inputs and comments on the draft report. These included: Artur Aleksanyan and Vladimir Aseyan of the Ministry of Finance of Armenia; Ali Hasanli and Nurlana Guliyeva of the Ministry of Economy of Azerbaijan; the Ministry of Economy, Ministry of Energy and Ministry of Natural Resources and Environmental Protection of Belarus; Nino Tkhilava and Venera Metreveli of the Ministry of Environmental Protection and Agriculture of Georgia; Mariana Botezatu, Consultant from Moldova. From Ukraine, we received valuable feedback from Volodymyr Tkachuk (National Energy and Utilities Regulatory Commission), Maryna Liudvenko (Ministry of Social Policy), Ivan Humeniuk (State Agency on Energy Efficiency and Energy Saving), Oleksii Voloshyn and Oleksandr Melnychenko (Secretariat of the Cabinet of Ministers of Ukraine), Borys Dodonov (Consultant).

Many OECD experts were involved at different stages of the project's implementation. Special thanks go to Mark Mateo, responsible for maintaining the OECD Fossil-Fuel Support Database, for his guidance on data collection and estimation and for his thoughtful observations on the draft. Jonas Teusch of the OECD Centre for Tax Policy and Administration, Talya Vatman of the International Energy Agency (IEA) and Angela Bularga of the European Commission also provided insightful comments and advice.

The authors would also like to thank Kumi Kitamori, Krzysztof Michalak, David Simek, Isabella Neuweg and Guy Halpern of the OECD Environment Directorate for their review and helpful comments on different versions of the report. Jonathan Wright provided overall administrative support for this work, as well as prepared the report for typesetting. Maria Dubois helped with preparing the report for publication, while Natalia Chumachenko translated the report into Russian. Mark Foss helped with editing the English version of the report.

Financial support from the European Union and Germany was vital for implementation of the project.

Table of contents

Tables

Figures

Boxes

Follow OECD Publications on:

http://twitter.com/OECD_Pubs

http://www.facebook.com/OECDPublications

http://www.linkedin.com/groups/OECD-Publications-4645871

http://www.youtube.com/oecdilibrary

http://www.oecd.org/oecddirect/

Abbreviations and acronyms

AMD	Armenian Dram
ASCM	Agreement on Subsidies and Countervailing Measures
AZN	Azerbaijani manat
BYN	Belarusian ruble
CHP	Combined heat and power
CNG	Compressed natural gas
CSE	Consumer Support Estimate
EAEU	Eurasian Economic Union
EaP	Eastern Partner / Eastern Partnership (countries)
EaP GREEN	The "Greening Economies in the EU's Eastern Neighbourhood" Project
EITI	Extractive Industries Transparency Initiative
EU	European Union
FF	Fossil fuels
FFSs	Fossil-fuel subsidies
GDP	Gross domestic product
GEL	Georgian lari
GNERC	Georgian National Energy and Water Supply Regulatory Commission
GSSE	General Services Support Estimate
IEA	International Energy Agency
JSC	Joint-stock company
LPG	Liquefied petroleum gas
MDL	Moldovan leu
n.a.	Not applicable
n.c.	Not calculated
n.d.	Not dated
NEURC	National Energy and Utilities Regulatory Commission of Ukraine
NJSC	National joint-stock company
NOGC	National oil and gas company
OECD	Organisation for Economic Co-operation and Development
PJSC	Public Joint-stock company
PPP	Purchasing power parity
PSE	Producer Support Estimate
SDG	Sustainable Development Goal
TES	Total energy supply
TPP	Thermal power plant
UAH	Ukrainian hryvnia
USD	United States dollar
VAT	Value-added tax
WTO	World Trade Organization

Executive summary

It is now well-documented that subsidies to fossil-fuel production and consumption distort costs and prices and lead to inefficiencies in the economy. In addition, the combustion of fossil fuels results in high levels of CO_2 and other greenhouse gas (GHG) emissions, as well as air pollution and related health problems. These can inflict a high cost on society.

Policy makers are now better informed and more aware of the negative fiscal, social, environmental and climate-related impacts of government support to fossil fuels. Therefore, reducing and reforming economically-inefficient and environmentally-harmful fossil-fuel subsidies has become a key issue on the political agenda of governments across the world. The significance of this agenda has risen particularly over the past ten years in the context of the international climate change debate and the shift to a low-carbon economy. Fossil-fuel subsidies, however, are still persistent and politically difficult to reform.

The European Union's Eastern Partner (EaP) countries – Armenia, Azerbaijan, Belarus, Georgia, Republic of Moldova (hereafter "Moldova") and Ukraine – are no exception. However, there is relatively little data availability and transparency on this issue in the EaP region. While fossil fuels continue to dominate the region's energy sector there is limited public discussion on the negative implications of government support to fossil fuels and possible benefits of its reform.

This report aims to fill the data gap and provide a basis for discussion on fossil-fuel subsidy reform in the EaP countries. These data are now available in the OECD database on government support to fossil-fuel production and consumption. The inclusion of the EaP countries in this database is an important milestone in achieving transparency. It recognises efforts of the EaP governments to disclose information on government support volumes that go to the energy sector in these countries.

The report analyses fossil-fuel subsidies provided to producers and consumers of coal, oil and related petroleum products (particularly in the transport sector), natural gas, as well as electricity and heat generated on the basis of these fossil fuels in the EaP countries. This analysis is an update of the 2010-15 subsidy estimates in the EaP region produced earlier by the OECD and covers the period 2016-19.

The current Inventory and this report focus on two major groups of subsidies: (i) direct transfers of funds to producers and consumers of fossil fuels; and (ii) tax expenditure (that is, reduction in tax liability compared with a "benchmark" tax system, such as the reduction or exemptions of value-added taxes [VAT] or excise taxes on fuel consumption). These two types of subsidies affect government budgets directly while other subsidies, such as those provided through setting tariffs at below-market price levels, are less visible to the population at large.

Major findings

Ukraine has the largest number of support measures

The analysis identified 65 measures of direct transfers of funds and tax expenditure (and revenue foregone) in the EaP countries. Ukraine has put in place the largest number of support measures (26) while Armenia has the smallest number (6). The other four countries have between seven and ten subsidies per country.

Fossil-fuel subsidies through budget transfers and revenue foregone declined in half of the countries

The mapping shows a distinct decline in fossil-fuel subsidies in the form of budget transfers and revenue foregone in Armenia, Georgia and Ukraine. Fossil-fuel subsidies in Armenia peaked in 2013 and 2014, reaching USD 42 million. They declined to USD 5 million in 2019 as most subsidy schemes were eliminated. In Georgia, quantified subsidies amounted to USD 33 million in 2013. They declined to USD 15 million in 2019, although new social support schemes were introduced in the meantime. In Ukraine, the cumulative value of budget transfers and tax expenditure surpassed USD 5 billion in 2012 but had declined by more than 50% by 2019. However, at USD 2.2 billion in 2019 the size of subsidy remains significant and is the largest among the EaP countries, including as a share of GDP. This suggests that Ukraine still has a long way to go in its energy subsidy reforms. Subsidy values in Moldova have fluctuated over the review period. Meanwhile, data gaps in the bottom-up assessment of fossil-fuel subsidies in Azerbaijan and Belarus preclude clearer conclusions on general trends.

Most EaP countries use budgetary transfers to subsidise fossil fuels

Budgetary transfers prevail in most EaP countries. In Moldova, tax expenditure is the main support mechanism. It takes the form of reduced VAT rates for natural gas, electricity and heating to households and public institutions, as well as for liquefied petroleum gas (LPG) consumption.

Ukraine and Azerbaijan have the largest amount of fossil-fuel subsidies as a share of GDP

In relative terms, when comparing annual fossil-fuel subsidies (budget transfers and tax expenditure) as a share of gross domestic product (GDP) with the national budget deficits in the EaP countries, Ukraine and Azerbaijan stood out in 2018. In Ukraine, fossil-fuel subsidies alone reached 2.3% of GDP, exceeding the 1.9% budget deficit. Similarly, in Azerbaijan, subsidies constituted almost 2% of GDP in 2018 and exceeded the 0.3% budget deficit. This represents an important potential for reform. Reducing fossil-fuel subsidies can lower the burden on the budget and can help reduce the budget deficit. Such savings can be re-allocated to other more urgent social and environmental priorities supported by the state.

Most subsidies target the residential sector and go to natural gas

Most subsidy measures support the residential sector, with a significant portion allocated to the oil and gas production sectors as well. Support to natural gas also features strongly; it is the main fuel used in generating electricity and heat in the region. Subsidies provided through below-market price tariffs often benefit all consumers in the residential sector and not only socially vulnerable households.

Energy pricing is still highly regulated in the EaP countries

Understanding fossil-fuel subsidies requires a good grasp of the underlying energy pricing and taxation policies as they are among the major channels for providing support to the energy sector. Energy pricing, and particularly energy tariffs, is highly regulated in the EaP countries. Keeping energy tariffs at below-market price levels encourages increased consumption of fossil fuels and gives rise to "indirect" subsidies that are more difficult to measure and reform. The market of liquid petroleum products is the most deregulated energy segment in the region. At the same time, the tax system in the countries has been rationalised and simplified. This, in turn, has led to increased tax collection and more transparent taxation practices

The policy landscape has changed and a number of reforms have been put in place

During the four years covered by the analysis, the landscape of fossil-fuel subsidies in the EaP countries has changed considerably. Several measures were eliminated, while new ones were introduced. Examples of such changes include:

- In 2016, Armenia phased out excise exemption for compressed natural gas worth around USD 9 million per year. A year later, it cancelled VAT exemption for diesel imports worth USD 17.6 billion.

- Belarus terminated VAT exemptions for natural gas and electricity for households in January 2016, ending a subsidy worth USD 200 million per year.
- Georgia's government introduced new budget transfers to provide gas subsidies for households living on the border of Abkhazia and South Ossetia. It also provided electricity subsidies for families with four and more children, and other socially vulnerable consumers and households living in high mountainous areas. Still, fossil-fuel subsidies in 2016-19 declined compared to the previous period of 2013-15 when subsidies peaked.
- Ukraine eliminated several budget transfers recently but, at the same time, introduced new ad hoc measures to deal with emergencies and arrears in the energy sector.

Major recommendations

Embrace a holistic approach to reform of fossil-fuel subsidies

Reforming fossil-fuel subsidies is crucial to reducing GHG emissions and hence meeting climate change goals. The governments in the region should build on reforms to date but need design further reforms more holistically. Fossil-fuel subsidies are usually a long-term problem that demand structural solutions. The reform has to be well-designed and its short- and longer-term consequences need to be clearly understood. Experience from many countries shows that targeted support measures (e.g. to vulnerable households) deliver better results and ensure better energy affordability than untargeted subsidies applicable to all. Transparency and stakeholder dialogue are the cornerstone of subsidy reforms.

Review recovery measures put in place in response to COVID-19

The COVID-19 crisis that hit in 2020 made countries painfully aware of the opportunity for reforming the subsidies. In response to the crisis, governments needed to mobilise significant additional funds to support their health systems and economies. The EaP governments reacted quickly and sought to protect their citizens and businesses by putting in place crucial rescue and recovery packages. The analysis shows that most such measures in the energy sector are largely concentrated in the end-use electricity sector. This is where countries and utilities have made commitments to avoid hardship during the crisis. These commitments include payment moratoria, late fee interest suspensions, additional assistance with bills or bans on disconnecting customers in arrears. The short-term justification for action is clear. However, governments must review the measures to ensure they do not develop into inefficient, longer-lasting subsidy programmes.

Undertake further study on "induced transfers"

The debate around energy subsidies in the EaP countries and their reforms is closely linked to keeping social tariffs below market prices. Any analysis would be incomplete without examining these "induced transfers". Such transfers usually involve regulations that mandate fossil-fuel companies to sell their products to certain categories of consumers (e.g. vulnerable households) at below-market prices. To complete the fossil-fuel subsidy picture, more analysis on induced transfers will be needed.

Improve reporting and transparency

Official government reporting on fossil-fuel subsidies in the EaP countries remains highly insufficient. Improving the transparency and credibility of data on fossil-fuel subsidies, including on tax expenditure in the energy sector, can help decision makers and the public at large design better reform measures. Such work can create significant value if undertaken by countries on their own.

Draw on this analysis for international reporting obligations

The EaP countries report on fossil-fuel subsidies within the frameworks of the United Nations Sustainable Development Goals (SDGs) and the World Trade Organization (WTO). They may wish to consider using data and estimates in this OECD analysis as a starting point for such reporting obligations.

1 Setting the scene

This chapter introduces some of the main issues that frame the analysis of and the debate on fossil-fuel subsidies and their reforms. It examines the need to monitor and measure fossil-fuel subsidies, including the difficulty of removing them once they are in place. Subsequently, it looks at drivers of fossil-fuel subsidy reform, including international frameworks such as the Sustainable Development Goals, the Paris Summit on Climate Change and the European Green Deal. Next, it discusses two complementary databases developed by the OECD and IEA to track government support to fossil-fuel production and consumption. The chapter ends with reflections on the COVID-19 crisis and its impact on energy markets and fossil-fuel subsidies.

Why monitor and measure fossil-fuel subsidies?

The debate on fossil-fuel subsidies has gained significant momentum over the past ten years. Governments are now better informed and more aware of the potentially negative fiscal, social, environmental and climate-related impacts of such subsidies on the economy.

Government support to fossil-fuel production and consumption has usually been used with the best of intentions. It generally aims to help the poor and ensure their access to affordable energy; to support rural and industrial development; to create jobs; and to ensure a country's energy security and energy independence. Often, however, end results could be different from intended outcomes.

As with all subsidies, fossil-fuel production and consumption subsidies distort costs and prices and lead to inefficiencies in the economy. Keeping energy prices low encourages more energy consumption. By encouraging use of fossil fuels and discouraging production of low-carbon fuels, such subsidies undermine the development and commercialisation of renewable energy and other alternative technologies. This, in turn, results in increased CO_2 and other greenhouse gas (GHG) emissions, as well as more stranded assets[1]. Combustion of fossil fuels leads to higher levels of air pollution and related health problems, which can inflict a high cost on society.

By now it is well-documented that untargeted consumer fossil-fuel subsidies often benefit the rich more than the poor (Javier et al., 2012[1]). On the production side, fossil-fuel subsidies often go to the largest and most economically powerful recipients, thus increasing profits for well-connected investors or industries. Indeed, lobbying and corrupt practices in the energy sector are ubiquitous.

Once introduced, many subsidy schemes may stay in place for a long time, unreformed and unremoved. As a result, they can become a significant drain on the public budget, leading to a substantial fiscal cost. They can also divert public funding from more urgent social priorities (such as health care or education) or from other cleaner sources of energy.

While fossil-fuel subsidies are popular and politically attractive, they are often difficult to reform or dismantle. Fossil-fuel subsidy reform is highly politicised, requiring high-level support and concerted efforts by the government. It must demonstrate strong political will and a long-term vision to take tough decisions that benefit society as a whole.

Investing time and resources to identify and measure fossil-fuel subsidies and the potential distributional effects of their reform and phase out can be useful. Such efforts may help policy makers make better informed decisions when they need to reform subsidies. Analysis can also help them explain subsidies and their impacts to all stakeholders. This is especially important to segments of the population that may be most negatively affected by the reform.

Fossil-fuel subsidy reform needs to be well-designed and its short and longer-term consequences need to be clearly understood. Experience from many countries shows that targeted support measures aimed e.g. at vulnerable households deliver better results and ensure better energy affordability than untargeted subsidies provided across the board. Transparency and stakeholder dialogue are the cornerstone of subsidy reform (OECD, 2013[2]). Awareness and understanding of subsidies based on credible data can improve transparency and inform decision making.

Much of the debate on fossil-fuel subsidy reform remains on an international level. The need for identifying and measuring fossil-fuel subsidies is often driven by international processes. Reforming and phasing out fossil-fuel subsidies lies at the heart of combating climate change and achieving net-zero emissions. However, none of the European Union's Eastern Partner (EU EaP) countries included such an objective in its Nationally Determined Contribution prepared for the Paris Summit on Climate Change in December 2015.

As a result of the various negative impacts of fossil-fuel subsidies, their reform was also turned into a Sustainable Development Goal (SDG). SDG 12 ("Ensure sustainable consumption and production patterns") and the related Target 12.c[2] and Indicator 12.c.1[3] focus on the rationalisation and phase-out of inefficient, economically wasteful and environmentally-harmful fossil-fuel subsidies (United Nations, 2017[3]). All governments are expected to report on progress in meeting the SDGs, including on the phase-out of fossil-fuel subsidies. Further, subsidies are an important issue in the framework of World Trade Organization (WTO) negotiations. WTO member countries, which includes most EaP countries, have committed to report on subsidies under the Agreement on Subsidies and Countervailing Measures (WTO, 1996[4]). When reporting on fossil-fuel subsidies within the SDG and WTO frameworks, the EaP countries may wish to use the data and estimates prepared in the current OECD analysis.

The European Green Deal (EC, 2019[5]) – the new EU growth strategy – sets a number of policy initiatives with the aim of making Europe climate neutral by 2050. Some of the main measures in the Green Deal include removing subsidies for fossil fuels and shifting the tax burden from labour to pollution, while considering social implications. The coronavirus pandemic has not diverted the European Union and its member states from their 2050 goal, but they will need to address the impact of COVID-19 on carbon pricing which can generate revenues to help finance green recovery measures. Carbon pricing can work hand-in-hand with green stimulus to promote clean investment and spending, and support a successful, long-term recovery (Pilichowski and Saint-Amans, 2020[6]). The European Union is also committed to reinforcing its support to the EaP countries to reduce fossil-fuel subsidies.

Fossil-fuel subsidy reform could be easier under international peer pressure and with access to lessons from other countries. The EaP countries could and should profit from these opportunities to push forward reforms in their countries.

OECD contribution to tracking down fossil-fuel subsidies

Over the years, the OECD has extensively analysed government support measures in both member countries and key emerging G20 economies (Brazil, the People's Republic of China, India, Indonesia, the Russian Federation, South Africa). Recently, the OECD and the International Energy Agency (IEA) launched two mutually exclusive but complementary online databases on government support to fossil-fuel production and consumption.[4] These databases are meant to be updated every other year.

The IEA and the OECD quantify fossil-fuel subsidies in different ways. The IEA applies the price-gap approach to estimate subsidies to consumers of coal, oil, natural gas and electricity. This measures the difference in the price of a specific energy carrier on domestic and international markets. For its part, the OECD uses a bottom-up approach. This involves constructing an inventory of policies supporting the production and consumption of energy, quantifying the value of support under each of them and then aggregating the numbers.

The OECD inventory addresses a broader range of measures, including many that do not directly reduce consumer prices below world market levels. It uses a broad concept of support that encompasses direct budgetary transfers and tax expenditure. These provide a benefit or economic advantage to fossil-fuel producers or consumers, either in absolute terms or relative to other activities or products.

In 2018, following both the OECD and IEA methodologies, the OECD Secretariat prepared an "*Inventory of Energy Subsidies in the EU's Eastern Partnership (EaP) Countries*" (hereafter "the EaP Inventory"). The EaP Inventory covered the six countries in the region – Armenia, Azerbaijan, Belarus, Georgia, Republic of Moldova (hereafter "Moldova") and Ukraine, and was prepared as part of the "Greening Economies in the EU's Eastern Neighbourhood" Project, funded by the European Union.

The EaP Inventory (OECD, 2018[7]), which covered 2010-15, was the first comprehensive and consistent record of energy subsidies in the region. The study provided quantitative estimates of government support made available to producers and consumers of coal, oil and related petroleum products and natural gas. It also accounted for electricity and heat generated on the basis of these fossil fuels. Further, the report briefly analysed public support allocated to energy-efficiency measures and renewable energy sources in the EaP countries. It also discussed the energy pricing and taxation policies that underpin the analysis of energy subsidies.

The 2018 analysis showed that while energy systems in the EaP countries had been reformed and restructured significantly, energy subsidies continued to play an important role in their energy policies. In 2010-15, all EaP countries supported fossil-fuel production and consumption. Most fossil-fuel subsidies aimed to benefit residential consumers. To that end, regulated energy prices set at below-market levels were the most important form of a subsidy in the EaP region. The bulk of subsidies went to natural gas. This was not surprising given that natural gas has dominated the energy mix in these countries for many years. It has also been used to generate electricity and heat.

Following this work, the OECD Secretariat decided to include information on existing fossil-fuel support measures in the EaP countries in the OECD-IEA fossil-fuel subsidies database. The inclusion of the EaP countries in this database is an important milestone in achieving transparency. It also recognises the efforts of the EaP governments to disclose information on government support volumes that go to the energy sector in these countries.

The impact of the COVID-19 crisis on energy markets and fossil-fuel subsidies

The COVID-19 crisis hit all countries hard with the health pandemic leading to a socio-economic crisis. All governments, as their first priority, sought to save the lives of their country's people and prevent their economies from sinking into a deep recession. To soften the consequences of this double crisis, governments have put in place recovery packages to support households and businesses.

The coronavirus pandemic has had a strong impact on global energy markets, contributing to a collapse in the price of oil, as well as lower prices for other fossil fuels. Global shutdowns of economic activity in 2020 led to sharply reduced energy consumption and lower energy-related GHG emissions.

Global energy demand in 2020 fell by 4%, the largest decline since World War II and the largest-ever absolute decline (IEA, 2021[8]). Oil and coal were hit particularly hard with demand dropping through the year by almost 9% and 4%, respectively. Demand for natural gas dropped by only 2%. While demand for all other fuels declined, use of renewable energy increased by 3% in 2020. This was largely due to more electricity generation from solar photovoltaics and wind, which grew by 12% and 23%, respectively.

As a result of the decline in energy demand, global CO_2 emissions decreased by 5.8% in 2020, which was called the largest-ever such decline in history (IEA, 2021[8]). However, demand for coal, oil and gas is expected to recover with the economy. Consequently, global energy-related CO_2 emissions are projected to rebound in 2021 and grow by 4.8%. This expected significant increase in emissions emphasises the need for further decarbonisation efforts and investments in cleaner and more resilient energy infrastructure.

As lockdown measures and travel bans led to a significant decline in global demand for energy, oil prices fell to unprecedentedly low levels. In March 2020, crude oil prices fell below zero for the first time in recorded history before recovering to more than USD 60 per barrel in April 2021.

The combination of low consumption and low oil prices wreaked havoc in energy markets. According to the IEA, oil and gas producers may have lost between 50% and 85% of their income in 2020. Lower oil prices are particularly damaging for countries that rely heavily on export revenues from oil production and whose public budgets depend on high oil prices.

The collapse in the price of oil at the beginning of the crisis led to lower prices of other fossil fuels as well. Sustained low oil prices could seriously damage gas producers that rely on linked contracts. However, low gas prices could facilitate switching to this fuel in industrial sectors that typically rely on coal use. These sectors range from steel and cement production to heating and electricity generation. The coronavirus pandemic led to a 25% decline in coal prices, making more of the industry unprofitable just as it faces severe criticism for its environmentally damaging effects (Wilson, 2020[9]).

Against the backdrop of relatively low fuel prices in 2020, COVID-19 negatively affected new energy investments in the energy sector. (IEA, 2020[10]) notes that "the speed and scale of the fall in energy investment activity in the first half of 2020 is without precedent". However, investments in renewables were a notable exception. They amounted to USD 359 billion in 2020, a 7% increase compared to 2019 levels (IEA, 2021[11]). The longer-term impact on investments will depend on the nature and speed of the economic recovery, as well as the differing responses of global policy makers to this challenge.

While the coronavirus pandemic had a visibly negative impact on the prices of fossil fuels, it also disrupted the supply of renewable energy equipment and technology. Though short-lived, the economic shutdown in the People's Republic of China in early 2020 led to disruption in the supply of solar panels, which are mainly produced in that country and exported globally. The combination of low fossil-fuel prices and serious economic difficulties could incite countries to review their investments in energy efficiency and renewable support schemes, particularly where these weigh significantly on government budgets (Wilson, 2020[9]).

When fossil-fuel prices are at historic lows, governments can seize the moment to phase out fossil-fuel subsidies. On the one hand, in a low-price environment, consumption subsidies are easier to reduce and countries could use this opportunity to reform them. On the other, when prices are low it is oil and gas producers that ask governments for help.

Low prices coupled with the pandemic lead to a different environment where citizens and companies may be less likely to object to the phase-out of subsidies. For example, citizens and companies may recognise that retaining subsidies will reduce the government's ability to provide for other urgent needs such as health care and economic stimulus. The crisis could thus offer an opportunity for governments to reallocate fiscal means to essential public services.

However, rolling back fossil-fuel subsidy reforms once oil prices are rising again would undermine reform. By the time the relevant reform packages are designed and ready for implementation, prices have often recovered. This makes it difficult to pursue successful reform.

Instead of using the low oil price argument, reform would be better discussed in the context of two other factors. First, reform could support the fight against climate change. Second, it could finance green stimulus measures by aligning traditional stimulus with climate objectives.

Governments that choose to phase out fossil-fuel subsidies should do so while considering their country's circumstances. The poorest are already suffering under the pandemic. Maintaining or better targeting support to them would likely reduce resistance to an overall fossil-fuel subsidy reform and also mitigate inequality effects. To retain citizen support for subsidy reform after the pandemic ends, governments should maintain visible improvements to health and other public services.

As governments move from the immediate emergency rescue phase into the stimulus and recovery stage, they have a real opportunity to make recovery packages greener. The phase-out of fossil-fuel subsidies together with carbon pricing and fuel taxation can help align price signals with and generate revenue for green recovery packages, as well as finance crisis-related debt.

References

EC (2019), *Communication from the Commission to the European Parliament, the European Council, the Council, the European Economic and Social Committee and the Committee of the Regions – The European Green Deal*, 11.12.2019, COM(2019) 640 Final, European Commission, Brussels, https://ec.europa.eu/info/sites/info/files/european-green-deal-communication_en.pdf. [5]

IEA (2021), *Global Energy Review 2021*, IEA, Paris, https://www.iea.org/reports/global-energy-review-2021. [8]

IEA (2021), *World Energy Investment 2021*, IEA, Paris, https://www.iea.org/reports/world-energy-investment-2021. [11]

IEA (2020), *World Energy Investment 2020*, IEA, Paris, https://www.iea.org/reports/world-energy-investment-2020. [10]

Javier, F. et al. (2012), "The unequal benefits of fuel subsidies: A review of evidence for developing countries", *World Development*, Vol. 40/11, pp. 2234-2248, https://doi.org/10.1016/j.worlddev.2012.05.005. [1]

OECD (2018), *Inventory of Energy Subsidies in the EU's Eastern Partnership Countries*, Green Finance and Investment, OECD Publishing, Paris, https://www.oecd.org/env/inventory-of-energy-subsidies-in-the-eu-s-eastern-partnership-countries-9789264284319-en.htm. [7]

OECD (2013), *Analysing Energy Subsidies in the Countries of Eastern Europe, Caucasus and Central Asia*, OECD Publishing, Paris, https://www.oecd.org/env/outreach/EHS%20report_20%20August%202013_ENG.pdf. [2]

Pilichowski, E. and P. Saint-Amans (2020), "COVID-19 and the climate crisis: Combining green budgeting and tax policy tools for a better recovery", OECD Environmental Focus blog, https://oecd-environment-focus.blog/2020/10/29/covid-19-and-the-climate-crisis-combining-green-budgeting-and-tax-policy-tools-for-a-better-recovery/. [6]

United Nations (2017), *Work of the Statistical Commission Pertaining to the 2030 Agenda for Sustainable Development, 71/313 General Assembly 71st session*, UN General Assembly, Geneva, https://undocs.org/A/RES/71/313. [3]

Wilson, A. (2020), "Impact of coronavirus on energy markets", *At a Glance*, No. PE 649.372, European Parliamentary Research Service, Brussels, https://www.europarl.europa.eu/RegData/etudes/ATAG/2020/649372/EPRS_ATA(2020)6493 72_EN.pdf. [9]

WTO (1996), *Agreement on Subsidies and Countervailing Measures*, World Trade Organization, Geneva, https://www.wto.org/english/docs_e/legal_e/24-scm_01_e.htm. [4]

Notes

[1] Stranded assets are physical assets recorded on a corporate balance sheet whose investment value cannot be recouped and must be written off. Their loss of value can be due to regulatory rulings that mean they cannot be exploited, changing trends in the market that renders them redundant, or obsolescence caused by superior technology.

[2] 12.c Rationalize inefficient fossil-fuel subsidies that encourage wasteful consumption by removing market distortions, in accordance with national circumstances, including by restructuring taxation and phasing out those harmful subsidies, where they exist, to reflect their environmental impacts, taking fully into account the specific needs and conditions of developing countries and minimizing the possible adverse impacts on their development in a manner that protects the poor and the affected communities (United Nations, 2017[3]).

[3] 12.c.1 Amount of fossil-fuel subsidies per unit of GDP (production and consumption) and as a proportion of total national expenditure on fossil fuels (United Nations, 2017[3]).

[4] For more information see: https://www.oecd.org/fossil-fuels/countrydata/.

2 Government support for fossil-fuel production and consumption in the Eastern Partner countries

This chapter summarises the main findings of the analysis of fossil-fuel subsidy schemes in the European Union's six Eastern Partner (EaP) countries (Armenia, Azerbaijan, Belarus, Georgia, Republic of Moldova and Ukraine). It introduces the methodology used to identify and estimate government support for fossil-fuel production and consumption. It also discusses some of the major fossil-fuel subsidy reforms that have been implemented in the EaP region since the first assessment of energy subsidies by the OECD. The chapter ends with the short-term responses of the EaP governments to the COVID-19 crisis in the energy sector and their possible impact on the evolution of fossil-fuel subsidies.

Subsidy identification and estimation methodology

Subsidy definition and classification

Each of the European Union's six Eastern Partner (EaP) countries (Armenia, Azerbaijan, Belarus, Georgia, Republic of Moldova and Ukraine) has its own legal and conceptual framework for energy pricing and taxation. These national contexts determine how the term "subsidy" is formally defined and understood in each country. OECD (2018[1]) discusses this issue in detail. Most EaP countries consider direct budget transfers to producers and consumers as a subsidy. The same is true for tax revenue foregone in terms of uncollected or under-collected levies on energy production and consumption. However, more often subsidies are called "state aid" or "state support".

The analysis in this report makes use of the OECD methodology for quantifying government support to fossil-fuel production and consumption (OECD, 2015[2]). This methodology has been developed through OECD's extensive work on analysing government support measures in both member countries and key emerging G20 economies (Brazil, the People's Republic of China, India, Indonesia, the Russian Federation and South Africa).

The OECD makes use of the most widely recognised definition, formulated in the Agreement on Subsidies and Countervailing Measures (ASCM) (WTO, 1996[3]) of the World Trade Organization (WTO).[1] It is also the only definition that is legally binding for all WTO member countries.

Under Article 1 and Article 2 of the ASCM, a subsidy is deemed to exist when the government renders support to a particular industry or company. More specifically, a subsidy exists when the government: i) provides direct transfer of funds or potential direct transfer of funds or liabilities; ii) forgoes or does not collect revenue that is otherwise due; iii) provides goods or services or purchases goods on terms that confer a benefit compared to market terms; and iv) provides income or price support.

Building on this definition, the OECD (2013[4]) classification groups subsidies into the following four categories:

- **direct transfers** of funds from the budget to energy producers and consumers (e.g. grants, support of energy purchases by low-income households)
- **tax expenditure and other government revenue foregone** (e.g. reduction or exemptions of certain taxes, such as value-added taxes [VAT] or excise taxes on fuel consumption)
- **induced transfers** (import tariffs, below-market electricity/heat prices, cross-subsidies in the electricity sector)
- **transfer of risk** to government (e.g. low-interest loans, loan guarantees).

The analysis follows the *OECD Inventory of Support Measures for Fossil Fuels*. This Inventory covers all OECD member countries, as well as a number of emerging economies. In contrast, the 2018 OECD *Inventory of Energy Subsidies in the EU's Eastern Partnership Countries* covered all four categories listed above and provided estimates for 2010-15. The current study covers the first two categories of subsidies only (i.e. direct transfers of funds and tax expenditure) and provides estimates for 2016-19. This means that estimates of total subsidies in the EaP countries in the two reviewed periods are not directly comparable.

These two categories of government support (i.e. direct transfers of funds and tax expenditure) are the backbone of the *OECD Inventory of Support Measures for Fossil Fuels* and the related OECD-International Energy Agency (IEA) fossil-fuel support database. "Induced transfers" are also included in the database as part of the IEA contribution to this work. In order to have the EaP countries included in the OECD-IEA database, emphasis is placed on analysing only direct transfers and tax expenditure.

Where appropriate, IEA data complement the analysis. The IEA produces annual estimates of fossil-fuel subsidies directed at consumers of coal, oil (petroleum products), natural gas and electricity in developing and emerging economies. These subsidy estimates reflect the difference between domestic and international prices of energy carriers. The IEA focuses on subsidies that directly affect end-user prices paid by consumers.

Direct budgetary transfers are the easiest and most straightforward to identify and measure as they are usually reported in government budgets, which are publicly available. Tax expenditure and other government revenues foregone (the monetary value of tax breaks) and induced transfers require significant data collection and additional estimation. This makes them more difficult to measure. The lack of established accounting and reporting practices of tax expenditure can limit their quantification. Difficulties with obtaining data that accurately represent the situation in countries with complex pricing systems for fuels and electricity is a major challenge when estimating induced transfers. Transfer of risk to government is a more complex issue. For this reason, volumes of this subsidy are quantified more rarely (OECD, 2013[4]).

Direct transfers and induced transfers are closely linked. Subsidies provided through regulated prices are not usually reported in government documents. This is why they are also referred to as "hidden" or "indirect" subsidies. All direct transfers of government funds to producers could reduce production costs, and therefore prices, in the medium- or long-term. When electricity or heat are provided to residential consumers at below-market tariffs, for example, someone else still pays the full price. Most often, the state covers the bill. In this case, the hidden subsidies can show as direct transfers to producers or consumers. However, this needs careful checking to make the correct links and avoid double-counting. Alternatively, cross-subsidies from industry to the population can be used.

The choice of the benchmark tax system is important to tax expenditure. Tax expenditure is the difference in revenue due to deviations from the tax norm (Kojima and Koplow, 2015[5]). Governments use several approaches to determine a benchmark tax regime. Many countries base their tax expenditure estimates on a conceptual view of "normal" taxation of income and consumption. Even in a relatively straightforward case such as the VAT, different approaches can lead to different results. Thus, some countries might see any tax rate lower than the standard VAT as generating tax "expenditure". Others might regard lower VAT rates as an inherent part of the tax system, which does not generate tax expenditure (OECD, 2013[4]). Tax expenditure estimates could increase either because of greater concessions relative to the benchmark tax treatment or because of a raise in the benchmark itself. This lack of a common benchmark does not allow straightforward comparisons across countries. International comparisons could be misleading due to country-specific benchmarks tax systems.

Data sources and data availability in the EaP countries

Data availability and fiscal transparency vary considerably across the six countries (Box 2.1) The analysis draws on a diverse body of publicly available sources of information. These include reports on budget execution and laws, reports of fiscal authorities and energy sector regulators, and any credible media sources. In most cases, subsidy values were collected at face value from government sources. When estimates of tax expenditure were not available, authors calculated revenue foregone using standard tax rates (e.g. VAT, excise taxes) as compared to preferential rates and amount of energy produced or consumed. Detailed, country-level fossil-fuel subsidy data collected and estimated are provided in Annexes B to G.

Box 2.1. Data availability and fiscal transparency in EaP countries

Government data sources

Different data availability across the EaP countries hinders consistent and comparable estimates of the magnitude of fossil-fuel subsidies and analysis of their reforms. The highest data transparency is observed in Ukraine where detailed information on budget expenditure and revenue foregone is available from publicly accessible sources. State Treasury Service of Ukraine (2020[6]) regularly publishes monthly, quarterly and annual reports on budget execution. These reports have sufficient data granularity for comprehensive analysis of fossil-fuel subsidies and consistent time series for the last ten years. The Ministry of Finance estimates revenue foregone due to major tax benefits. This is often published in a package of budget planning documents attached to draft budget laws (see for example (Ministry of Finance of Ukraine, 2020[7]).

Comprehensive data are less readily available in Armenia, Georgia and Moldova. However, they are still sufficient to build a credible picture when supplemented by direct contact with government agencies and authors' own estimates. The most difficult situation with data availability is in Azerbaijan and Belarus. In these two countries, data gaps, inconsistency and unavailability mean findings can only indicate trends in fossil-fuel subsidies. They should be interpreted with this limitation in mind.

The Budget and Tax Codes of Azerbaijan and Belarus establish the legal basis for state support in the form of budget transfers and tax benefits. However, limited information on the magnitude of such measures is publicly available. The government of Azerbaijan does not publish data on budget spending or revenue foregone in the energy sector (OECD, 2018[1]). Though Belarus publishes reports on budget execution, data are available at a high level (e.g. category "fuel and energy") without details about spending on particular government programmes. Budget laws and passports of state programmes in the energy sector provide more information, but it is often unclear how much of the planned budgets have been spent.

International data sources

Participation in the Extractive Industries Transparency Initiative (EITI) helps increase transparency and strengthen governance of extractive industries, including the energy sector. Among the six EaP countries, only Ukraine and Armenia are EITI members. Since joining EITI in 2013, Ukraine has published three national reports demonstrating meaningful progress in adhering to the EITI standard (EITI, 2020[8]). The EITI National Report of Ukraine provides, among others, information on budget programmes in the coal, and oil and natural gas sectors, state guarantee obligations and quasi-fiscal operations in the energy sector (EY, 2018[9]). The first report of Armenia, which joined EITI in 2017, focused on the metal and mineral mining sector as there is virtually no domestic energy production (EITI, 2020[10]). Azerbaijan joined EITI in 2007 and withdrew in March 2017 following suspension from the EITI Board due to limited progress in meeting the corrective actions related to civil society (EITI, 2018[11]).

Approaches to subsidy measurement

There are two main approaches to quantifying subsidies. A top-down approach prepares estimates based on price-gap assumptions, while a bottom-up approach constructs inventories that consider each government support measure individually. Each approach has its strengths and limitations, and the two can complement each other. This complementarity is especially useful when access to data and subsidy reporting is restricted (OECD, 2018[1]).

29

The **price-gap method** compares end-use prices paid by consumers with reference prices that correspond to the full cost of energy supply: a subsidy is present if the end-use price falls short of the reference price. The general stylised application of this approach consists of two main steps: i) calculating the price gap (Price gap = Reference price – End-user price); and ii) calculating the subsidy value (Subsidy = Price gap × Units of consumed energy).

For net energy importers of fossil fuels, reference prices (or international benchmark market prices) of fossil fuels are based on the import parity price.[2] For net exporters of fossil fuels, reference prices are based on the export parity price.[3] For energy exporters, the quantified subsidy represents the opportunity cost of selling fuels at below-market prices domestically rather than a measure of direct expenditure (OECD, 2018[1]).

The IEA uses the price-gap approach to produce its consumer subsidy estimates. This approach is useful to make comparisons possible across countries where the main form of support is provided through administrative pricing or export restrictions. However, this method fails to capture subsidies that are not revealed through the examination of price differentials.

The **inventory approach** used by the OECD can capture the subsidies that are not revealed by the top-down price-gap method. Through its bottom-up approach to quantifying subsidies, the OECD method constructs an inventory of policies that support the production and consumption of energy, quantify the value of support under each of them and then aggregate the numbers.

These two approaches are not mutually exclusive. Rather, they complement each other by looking at the same phenomenon from two different angles. OECD (2018[1]) discusses these approaches in detail.

Quantified fossil-fuel subsidies and pace of fossil-fuel subsidy reforms in the EaP countries

Analysis of the key results of fossil-fuel subsidy estimates in the EaP countries

Table 2.1 summarises estimates of recent fossil-fuel subsidies in the form of budget transfers and tax expenditure in the EaP countries during the period 2010-19 in line with the scope of the *Inventory* (see Annexes B-G for more details). Some of the totals for 2010-15 reported in OECD (2018[1]) may be different from the numbers in Table 2.1. This is primarily explained by differences in the scope of the Inventory over the two reviewed periods. In addition, this current study has identified new measures for the previous period and updated some of the previously-identified estimates as well.

This difference between 2010-15 data and numbers in Table 2.1 is particularly true for Azerbaijan. Recent data collected for this study and availability of additional data helped to cover several gaps on subsidy values in Azerbaijan. However, Azerbaijan's subsidies for both natural gas and electricity consumption for 2010-15 were estimated indirectly through the price-gap approach. Consequently, the previous and current assessments are not comparable.

In addition, most EaP countries have experienced significant currency depreciation in recent years (see Annex A for exchange rates). Thus, care should be taken when using USD estimates to assess changes in magnitude. Finally, the values of the quantified fossil-fuel subsidies are not directly comparable across countries as each country has its own tax benchmarks.

There may also be some differences in the subsidy values reported in this report and the values included in the OECD online database. This mostly concerns subsidy schemes which (i) benefit more than one economic sector/fuel (e.g. one single subsidy provided to consumers of coal, natural gas and oil products) or (ii) end-use electricity where it is generated not only from fossil-fuel sources (e.g. renewables and nuclear) or is imported.

In the database, the disaggregation by type of fuel is undertaken in case i while the subtraction of the non-fossil-fuel component and/or imported electricity from the electricity subsidy value is performed in case ii. This disaggregation is done using the IEA Energy Balance flows (IEA, 2020[12]) (Annex I). The disaggregation ensures consistency with the reporting of subsidy values in the database for the OECD countries.

This study reports non-disaggregated subsidy values for two main reasons. First, analysis shows that disaggregation by different types of fuel based on the IEA balances may lead to underestimation of the fossil-fuel component in subsidy values. Second, raw data in official government documents make it easier for countries to understand and trace these subsidies back to the original sources of information.

Table 2.1. Quantified fossil-fuel subsidies in EaP countries, budget transfers and tax expenditure, 2010-19, USD million

	2010	2011	2012	2013	2014	2015	2016	2017	2018	2019
Armenia	28	37	41	42	42	32	23	23	5	5
Azerbaijan	90	501	180	390	48	474	1 214	0.1	909	798
Belarus	594	160	197	303	318	18	71	110	85	81
Georgia	7	7	11	33	31	27	18	14	15	15
Moldova	72	89	100	93	83	66	60	65	72	n.c.
Ukraine	2 109	2 623	5 196	3 157	2 503	1 182	1 989	2 999	2 976	2 230
Total	2 900	3 417	5 725	4 017	3 026	1 799	3 374	3 210	4 061	3 128

Notes:
a. n.c.: Not calculated.
b. These estimates are affected by data availability for different years and by currency exchange rates.
Source: Based on country estimates presented in Annexes A-G.

Figure 2.1 illustrates how the cumulative value of fossil-fuel subsidies in the EaP region evolved over the period 2010-19. The overall dollar value of fossil-fuel subsidies in Ukraine is larger than in the five other EaP countries combined. In addition to having the largest economy, Ukraine has a strong legacy of subsidising its energy sector and population. It traditionally comes out on top in terms of fossil-fuel subsidies relative to gross domestic product (GDP). However, it also performs best on data transparency, which allowed identification and collection of data on all major subsidy schemes at the national level. The chance of under-reporting, then, is significantly lower for Ukraine than for the other countries.

Figure 2.1. Quantified fossil-fuel subsidies in EaP countries compared to the previous estimate, USD million

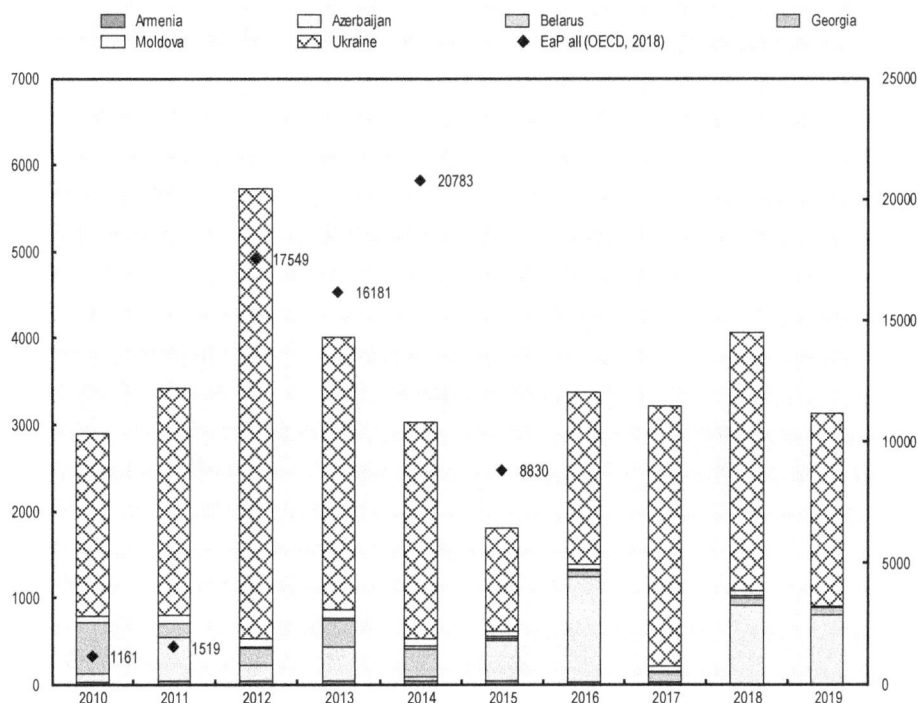

Note: Based on estimates presented in Annexes A-G and (OECD, 2018[1]). Data on the EaP all (OECD, 2018[1]) are indicated on the right axis.

Fossil-fuel subsidies in the form of budget transfers and revenue foregone have been decreasing in Armenia, Georgia and Ukraine starting in 2012-13 (Table 2.1). Fossil-fuel subsidies in Armenia peaked in 2013 and 2014, reaching USD 42 million. They declined to USD 5 million in 2019 as most subsidy schemes were phased out. In Georgia, subsidies grew from 2010, reaching USD 33 million in 2013. They have since declined to USD 15 million in 2019, although new social schemes were introduced.

In Ukraine, the cumulative value of budget transfers and tax expenditure amounted to more than USD 5 billion in 2012. This declined by more than half by 2019. However, it still exceeds USD 2 billion and is 2.4 times the total of the remaining countries. Subsidy values in Moldova fluctuated over the reviewed period. Data gaps in the bottom-up assessment of fossil-fuel subsidies in Azerbaijan and Belarus make it difficult to observe a clear general trend.

To complement the bottom-up analysis applied by the earlier OECD study (2018[1]), the current study also used the price-gap approach employed by the IEA. Unfortunately, an independent price-gap analysis falls beyond the scope of this report. IEA estimates are available only for Azerbaijan (Figure 2.3) and Ukraine (Figure 2.3).

The price-gap approach estimates subsidies to end-consumers of fossil fuels and electricity. To that end, it compares average end-user prices with international reference or market prices. The approach typically demonstrates how policy interventions lower the price for end-users below market levels.

For Azerbaijan, IEA subsidy estimates dropped in 2014-16. This reflected a sharp increase of domestic prices for petroleum products and natural gas coupled with the deterioration of the oil and gas world market prices. The value of fossil-fuel subsidies then bounced back. They exceeded even previous levels as petrol prices in USD remained unchanged from the end of 2017 until now (Trade Economics, 2020[13]) while world prices recovered. Consumer subsidies in Azerbaijan reached USD 2.6 billion in 2018, which is equivalent to 5.8% of GDP (IEA, 2019[14]).

Figure 2.2. IEA estimates of fossil-fuel subsidies in Azerbaijan, real 2018 USD billion

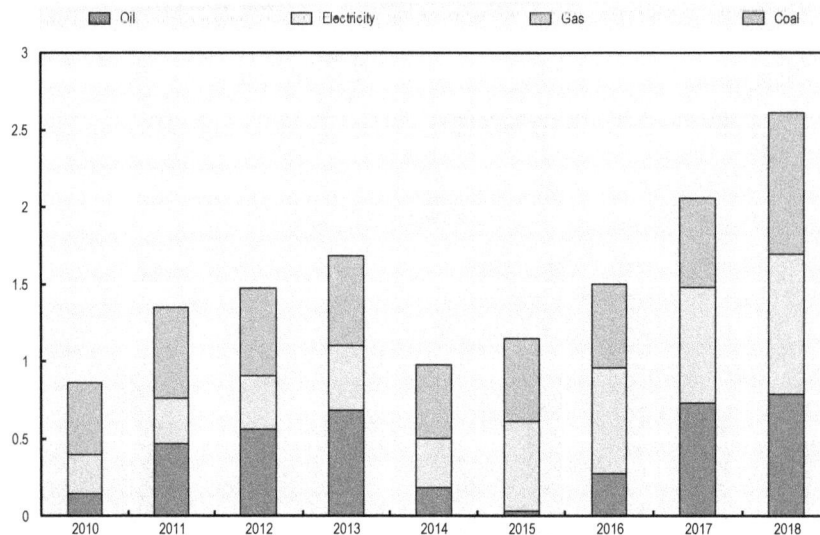

Source: Based on (IEA, 2019[14]) data.

IEA price-gap estimates for Ukraine (Figure 2.3) also reflect a combination of domestic and external factors. The introduction of import price parity (international market price) in domestic gas pricing formulae in 2016 led to increased tariffs. Consequently, "blanket" consumer subsidies in the gas sector were effectively removed for two years. The lowest level of consumer subsidies was observed in 2017 (USD 2.1 billion), and only in electricity production. In 2018, consumer subsidies re-emerged in the gas sector because the government was reluctant to increase domestic prices to reflect changes in international market prices (Ekonomichna Pravda, 2018[15]).

Figure 2.3. IEA estimates of fossil-fuel subsidies in Ukraine, real 2018 USD billion

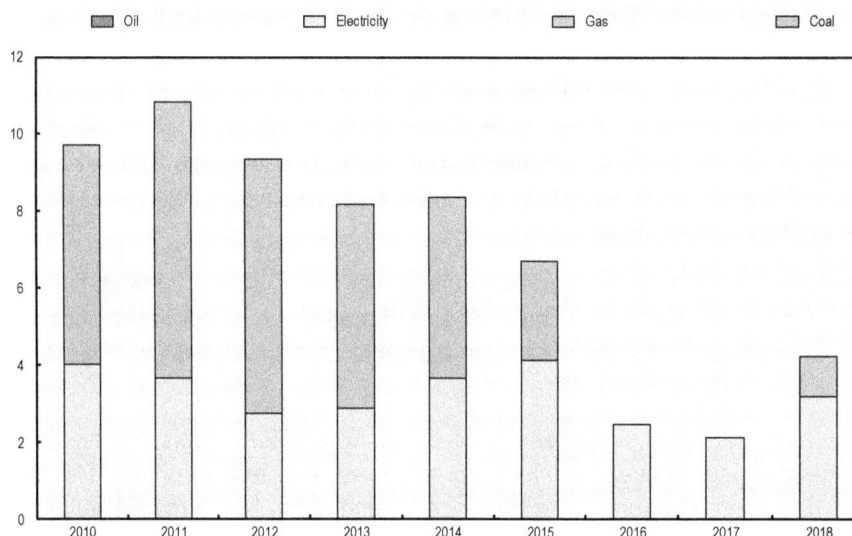

Source: Based on (IEA, 2019[14]) data.

Step-wise increases of electricity tariffs for households in Ukraine helped narrow the gap with the market price (IEA, 2019[14]) from 2015 to 2017 (NEURC, 2016[16]). However, electricity tariffs were not revised until 2021[4], resulting in a subsidy increase in 2018. In 2018, the total value of consumer subsidies in the gas and electricity sectors reached USD 4.2 billion, corresponding to 3.4% of GDP.

Box 2.2. Debt of subsidised national oil and gas companies

National oil and gas companies (NOGCs) exist in both Azerbaijan (SOCAR) and Ukraine (Naftogaz). These are state-owned vertically integrated companies that perform a full cycle of operations – from exploration and exploitation of oil and gas to refining and supply (OECD, 2018[11]). In both countries, the state supports the companies through cash contributions, equity injections, loan guarantees and issuance of state bonds to cover their deficits. Direct transfers to both companies have been identified. However, loan guarantees or issuance of bonds, which generate subsidy and represent transfer of risk to government, are more difficult to identify and measure.

NOGCs are often highly indebted, creating broader fiscal risks even if the state does not formally guarantee debts. When guaranteed by the state, such debt qualifies as a fossil-fuel subsidy. Figure 2.4 shows the level of debt as a share of government gross debt of several NOGCs in the region, including in Azerbaijan and Ukraine, over 2016-18.

After the 2016 gas pricing reform, Naftogaz stopped receiving direct budgetary support to compensate for its losses. In the same year, the company took a loan from the World Bank worth USD 500 million under state guarantees to support liquidity. The loan was fully repaid in May 2019. The value of Naftogaz state-guaranteed debt peaked at UAH 28 912 million (USD 1 132 million) in 2016. It dropped to UAH 2 694 million (USD 96 million) in 2019 (Naftogaz of Ukraine, 2016[17]), (Naftogaz Group, 2019[18]). The share of Naftogaz state-guaranteed debt decreased to 5% at the end of 2019. This was down from 28% at the end of 2018 due to repayment of the World Bank loan in 2019 (Fitch Ratings, 2020[19]).

The level of indebtedness of the Azerbaijani company SOCAR is particularly high. In 2018, it was more than twice the level of government gross debt. The state guarantees 9% of the company's debt and provides equity injections to cover its cash deficits (Fitch Ratings, 2020[20]).

Figure 2.4. NOGC debt/government gross debt, percentage

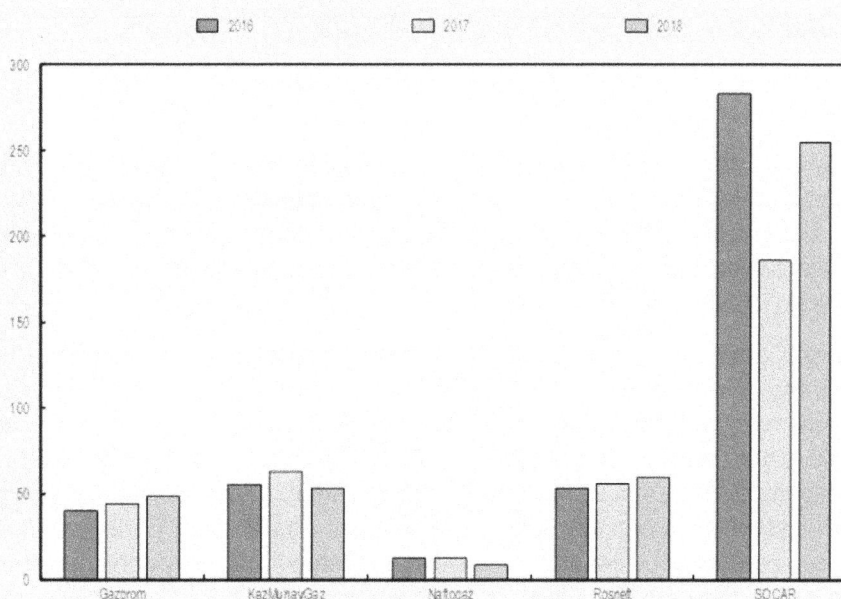

Source: Based on National Oil Company Database, (Natural Resource Governance Institute, 2020[21]).

Figure 2.5 presents annual fossil-fuel subsidies (budget transfers and tax expenditure) as a share of GDP, comparing them with national budget deficits in the EaP countries in 2018. In Ukraine, fossil-fuel related budget transfers and tax expenditure alone reached 2.3% of GDP, exceeding the 1.9% budget deficit. In Azerbaijan, subsidies constitute almost 2% of GDP, while the budget deficit is limited to 0.3% of GDP. In all other EaP countries, except Belarus where the budget was in surplus, budget deficits are larger; subsidies constitute less than 1% of GDP. Reducing fossil-fuel subsidies can lower the burden on the budget and reduce the budget deficit. Such savings can be re-allocated to more urgent state-supported social and environmental priorities.

Figure 2.5. General government deficit/surplus and quantified fossil-fuel subsidies as a share of GDP in 2018

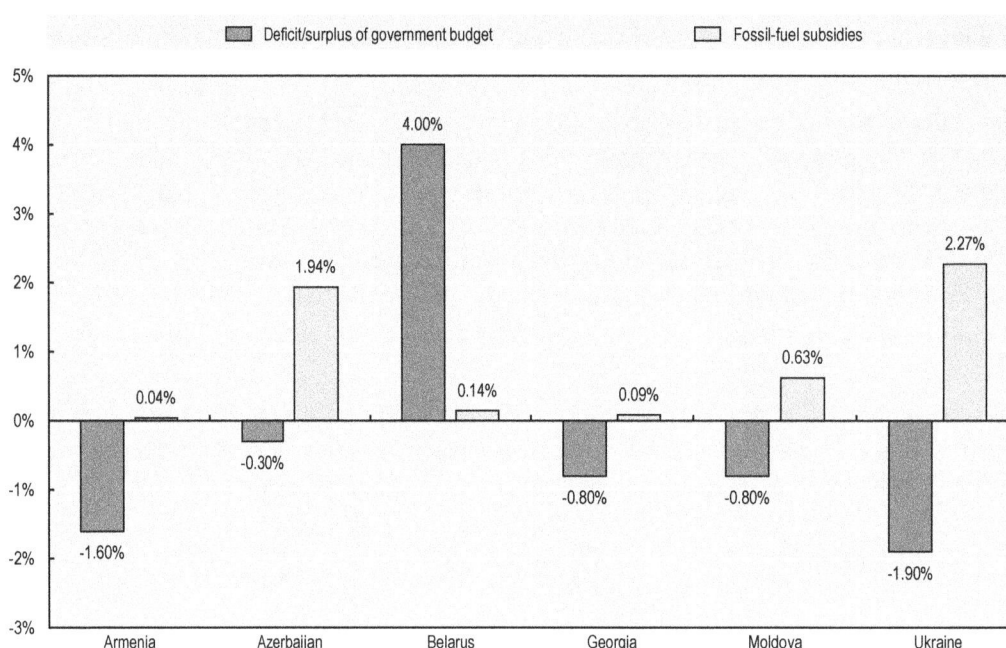

Source: Based on Eurostat (2019[22]) and World Bank (2020[23]) data and subsidy estimates presented in Table 2.1.

Figure 2.6 further breaks down the 2018 values of the quantified fossil-fuel subsidies by fuel in the EaP countries. In most cases, it is not possible to accurately disaggregate subsidy values by type of fuel. This is due both to data limitations and the possibility of a subsidy scheme to benefit several fuels (Annexes B-G).[5] A considerable share of support is allocated to natural gas and electricity. During the reviewed period, coal subsidies were significant only in Ukraine.

A study by the Energy Community (Miljević, 2020[24]) analysed direct subsidies to coal and lignite electricity production in the Energy Community Contracting Parties over the period 2018-19. The study confirmed that of all EaP members of the Energy Community (Georgia, Moldova and Ukraine) only Ukraine provides subsidies to electricity generated from coal. While data on direct budgetary support that come from the budget execution reports of the Treasury of Ukraine are consistent in both reports, the Energy Community analysis is broader and includes estimates on, among others, low-interest loans and loans guarantees extended to electricity producers by the state. Subsidies provided in this way constitute transfer of risk to government and a longer term liability to the state and are not covered by the OECD study. The Energy Community analysis shows a significant increase in subsidies for coal-fired electricity in Ukraine in 2019 (about 60%) compared to 2018.

Figure 2.6. Quantified fossil-fuel subsidies in EaP countries by fuel in 2018, USD million

Several fuels   Electricity   LPG   Oil & oil products   Natural gas   Coal and peat

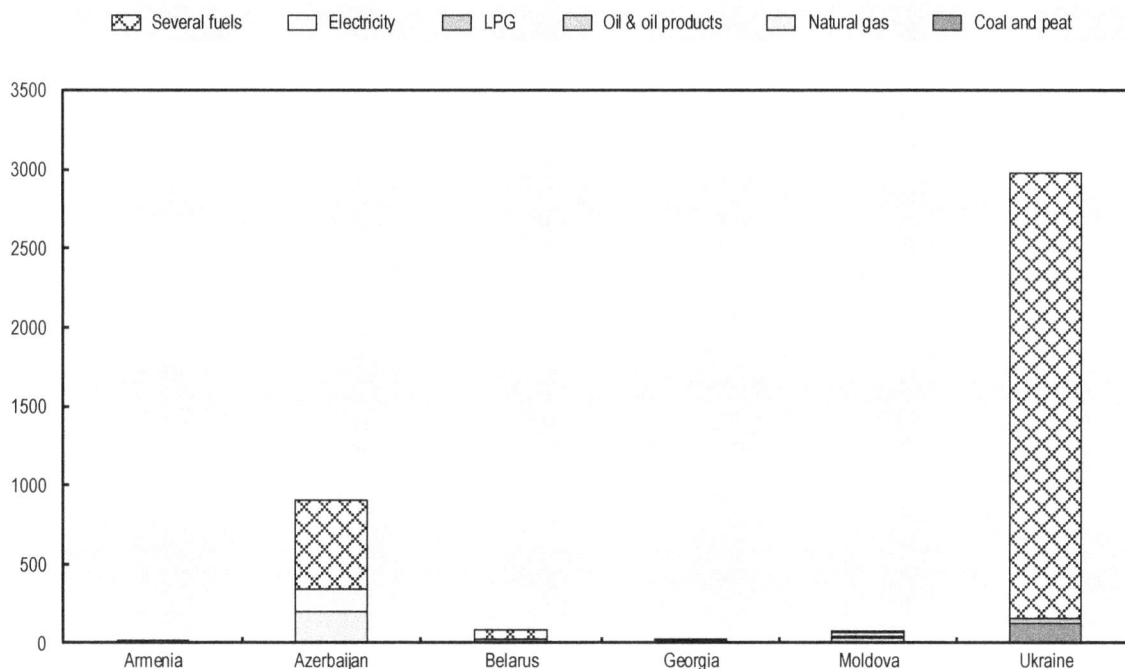

Source: Based on estimates presented in Annexes B-G.

Budget transfers and revenue foregone

The period 2015-19 has seen considerable changes to fossil-fuel subsidies in the EaP countries. Many measures have been eliminated as new ones have been introduced. Figure 2.7 illustrates that budget transfers prevail in most EaP countries; tax expenditure is the main mechanism of support only in Moldova.

Tax expenditure in Moldova was channelled to households and public institutions through reduced VAT rates for consumption of natural gas, electricity and heating, and liquefied petroleum gas (LPG). In 2018, the total value of these tax benefits in Moldova was estimated at USD 65.6 million. Meanwhile, budget spending on partial compensation of energy resources costs to households in Chisinau and on the Transnistria border reached roughly USD 6 million. Detailed information on budget transfers and revenue foregone in the EaP countries is provided in Annexes B-G.

The analysis revealed limited subsidies in Armenia, which do not appear to create significant distortions in energy consumer choices. Most subsidies were eliminated. At the end of 2019, only two subsidy schemes remained. These were budget transfers on partial compensation of costs for electricity and gas consumption for border communities; and excise tax exemption on natural gas imports.[6] Armenia phased out excise exemption for compressed natural gas worth around USD 9 million per year in 2016. A year later, it cancelled VAT exemption for diesel imports worth USD 17.6 billion.

Belarus terminated a VAT exemption for electricity and natural gas for households in January 2016, ending a subsidy worth USD 200 million per year. Azerbaijan has VAT and custom duties exemptions under so-called Production Sharing Agreements and Host Government Agreements. However, information on conditions of such exemptions and the magnitude of support is not publicly available.

Between 2014 and 2019, Georgia introduced new budget transfers to subsidise gas and electricity consumption. The gas subsidies targeted households on the border of Abkhazia and South Ossetia. Meanwhile, it provided electricity subsidies for families with four and more children, other socially vulnerable consumers and households living in high mountainous areas. Still, subsidies are declining; the total value of subsidies in GEL peaked in 2015 and in USD value in 2013.

Ukraine has recently eliminated several budget transfers, while introducing *ad hoc* measures to deal with emergencies and arrears. It introduced a transfer to Smilakomunteploenergo (Town of Smila Communal Heat Energy Utility) to prevent an emergency due to the utility's inability to pay for natural gas. Ukraine had three tax expenditure measures in effect as of 2019. In 2011, it introduced excise tax relief for operations on the sale of LPG at specialised auctions for the needs of households. In 2016, VAT relief for supply of coal and/or products of its enrichment on the customs territory of Ukraine was introduced. Finally, in 2018 and 2019, Ukraine provided a corporate income tax credit for the amount of excise tax levied on heavy distillates (gasoil) used in transport vehicles. The Ministry of Finance estimated that these measures led to foregone revenue of USD 141 million in 2019.

Figure 2.7. Quantified fossil-fuel subsidies in EaP countries by type of support measure in 2018, USD million

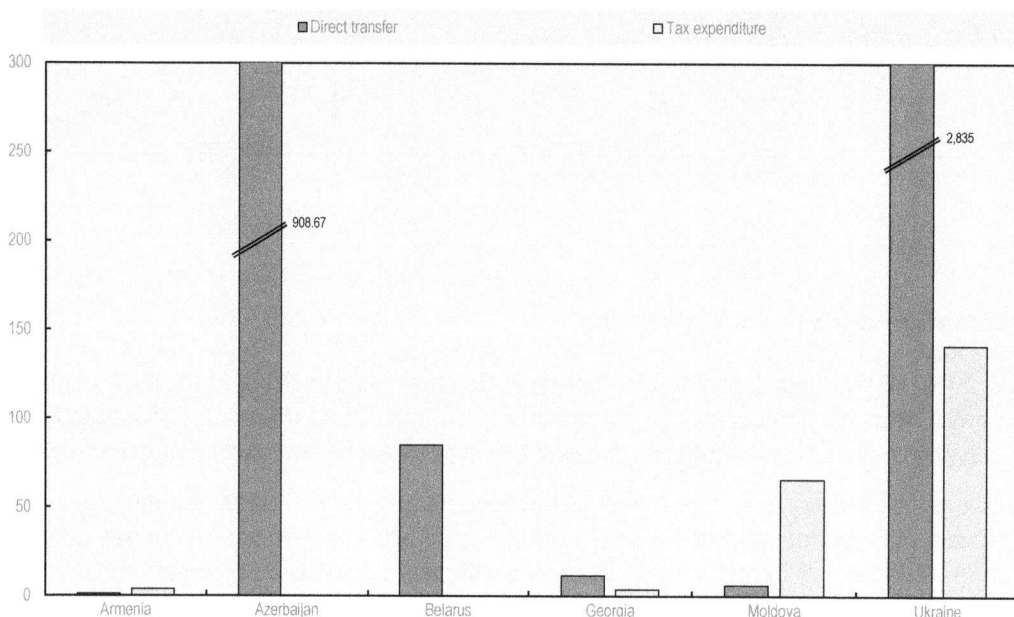

Source: Based on estimates presented in Annexes A-G.

Producer and consumer support estimates

Depending on the end-beneficiary, the OECD classifies measures as Consumer Support Estimate (CSE), Producer Support Estimate (PSE) and General Services Support Estimate (GSSE). The first category refers to measures, which benefit individual consumers. The second category refers to individual producers. The third one refers to measures that benefit both consumers and producers collectively as "measures that do not increase current production or consumption of fossil fuels but may do so in the future" (OECD, 2015[2]).

Figure 2.8 illustrates the breakdown of quantified fossil-fuel subsidies in the EaP countries under the OECD's PSE-CSE accounting framework. The GSSE measure was observed only in Moldova in the form of public investment in natural gas pipelines and electricity grids, which peaked at USD 7.3 million in 2014. It is not shown on Figure 2.8 as data for 2018 are not available.

Figure 2.8. Quantified fossil-fuel subsidies in EaP countries by PSE/CSE indicator, 2018, USD million

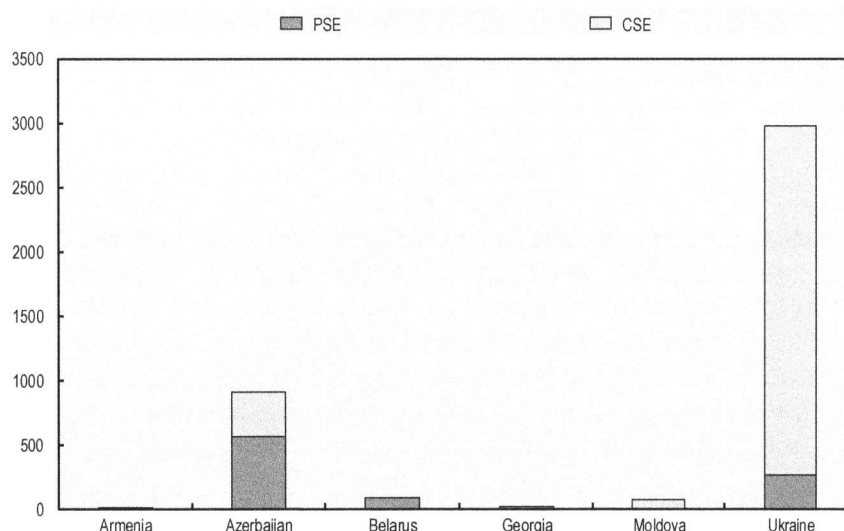

Source: Based on estimates presented in Annexes A-G.

All identified and quantified subsidies in Armenia and Moldova belong to the CSE category. In Belarus, the situation is reversed – all estimated fossil-fuel subsidies in 2018 benefit individual producers. CSE measures in Belarus include housing subsidies for low-income households and partial compensation of costs of utility providers. However, data on the magnitude of such support schemes have not been publicly reported. Therefore, these measures are excluded from the quantified analysis.

The PSE and CSE subsidy estimates for Azerbaijan show stable transfers to the country's energy utility companies and commensurate amounts of support to refugees and internally displaced persons.

Government support for fossil fuels in Georgia targets consumers through social subsidies and benefits, allocated directly to households. The government of Georgia supports keeping tariffs low for all households for social and political reasons. However, it has gradually reformed its social support programmes to target eligible low-income households. The PSE subsidy is concentrated in the oil and gas sector to facilitate production of local energy resources. Oil and gas producers are exempt from profit tax, property tax and fees for the use of natural resources.

The bulk of government support for fossil fuels in Ukraine targets consumers. This takes the form of budgetary transfers to cover losses of utility providers due to regulated below-market tariffs; or social subsidies and benefits allocated directly to households.

Producer support in Ukraine is concentrated in the coal sector. Various budget transfers have supported inefficient and unprofitable state-owned coal mines. Total PSE dropped after 2013 (see Annex G) for two reasons. First, the government lost temporary control of territories in the Donbass region where most state-owned coal mines in Ukraine are located. Second, on a smaller scale, reforms in the coal sector also led to a drop in PSE.

In 2018, the government discontinued allocation of budget funds to the "State Programme on Prevention and Elimination of Emergencies at Coal Mines" and for partial compensation of production costs of finished marketable coal. The latter measure had been provided to unprofitable coal mines for 15 years. A year earlier, in 2017, the government ended the "State Programme on the Improvement of Safety Measures at Coal Mining Enterprises", which was in place since 2005. At the same time, it introduced new budget programmes to finance the decommissioning of unprofitable coal and peat mining enterprises and the repayment of electricity arrears on behalf of state-owned coal-mining enterprises.

All EaP countries have various social support measures to support vulnerable households. Most of these were introduced in the 1990s (OECD, 2018[1]). Box 2.3 describes the reform of utility subsidies for vulnerable households in Ukraine.

Box 2.3. Reform of utility subsidies for low-income households in Ukraine

Given that utility tariffs were traditionally kept relatively low (well below cost-recovery levels) and the application procedure for targeted support was complicated, the number of subsidy beneficiaries was not large. In 2014, 1.2 million households received utility subsidies (Voitko, 2015[25]). The overall cost of these targeted subsidies on the national budget was lower, for example, than that of transfers of funds to the coal sector. Over 2012-14, Ukraine's government allocated USD 519-841 million for partial compensation of low-income households for utility payments and a further USD 60-92 million for the purchase of LPG, solid and liquid furnace fuel (State Treasury Service of Ukraine, 2020[6]).

As utility tariffs increased during 2015-17 so did the funds allocated for targeted subsidies to low-income households. To ease the administration of subsidy programmes, the government took several measures. It simplified procedures for allocating subsidies, reduced the number of documents required for submission in 2016 and cancelled several eligibility requirements. This led to a dramatic increase in applications for subsidies. The total value of utility subsidies to households peaked at USD 2.7 billion in 2017 (UAH 72 billion, see Annex G.). Furthermore, in this same year, 9.6 million households received utility subsidies, which is 64% of all households in Ukraine (State Statistics Service of Ukraine, 2018[26]), (State Statistics Service of Ukraine, 2019[27]).

In subsequent years, Ukraine amended subsidies to improve means-testing and ensure that subsidies are provided only to truly socially vulnerable households. By 2019, together with a general improvement in the economic situation in Ukraine, these measures led to a significant decrease in the number of households receiving benefits. Their number dropped to 5.9 million or about 40% of all households in the country (State Statistics Service of Ukraine, 2019[28]), (State Statistics Service of Ukraine, 2020[29]). Budget spending on housing subsidies dropped to USD 1.9 billion in total, which is comparable to the 2016 level when utility tariffs had just been sharply increased.

In March 2019, Ukraine's government further reformed utility subsides, implementing the so-called monetisation of subsidies. This reform allowed recipients to receive support for utility payments in cash or at specially opened bank accounts (Ministry of Social Policy of Ukraine, 2019[30]). In previous arrangements, the consumer's utility bill indicated the amount of subsidy, but compensation from the budget was transferred to utility providers. The new mechanism provided incentives for households to implement energy-saving measures as they are allowed to spend saved subsidies as they wish. Despite concerns about non-payment, subsidy beneficiaries demonstrated good payment discipline (Center of Public Monitoring and Control of Ukraine, 2019[31]).

Source: Authors' compilation.

Over the period 2015-19, the landscape of fossil-fuel subsidies in the EaP countries has changed considerably. Many measures were eliminated, while new ones were introduced. The analysis shows that fossil-fuel subsidies in the form of budget transfers and revenue foregone in Armenia, Georgia and Ukraine have generally declined over the reviewed period. Meanwhile, subsidy values in Moldova have fluctuated. Given data gaps in the bottom-up assessment of fossil-fuel subsidies in Azerbaijan and Belarus, the study could not identify general trends in these countries.

Measures related to COVID-19 in the energy sector of the EaP countries

The COVID-19 pandemic has taken a heavy toll on the global economy, including the EaP region. COVID-19 has adversely affected the EaP countries through the collapse in global commodity prices, disruptions to global and regional supply chains, and increased risk aversion in financial markets. The spread of the virus and the subsequent lockdown has led to a steep decline in domestic demand and halted much activity.

The pandemic reached the EaP region in late February 2020. By the end of July 2020, infection rates had significantly increased. At the end of April 2021, the numbers of confirmed cases were further increasing. In terms of numbers of confirmed cases, Ukraine appears to be the most affected country in the region. However, Armenia, Georgia and Moldova display high rates in terms of per capita deaths as well. All EaP countries have been struggling to contain the health crisis over the past year.

Table 2.2. Infections and deaths per capita, as of 26 July 2020 and 30 April 2021

	Confirmed cases, 26 July 2020	Confirmed cases, 30 April 2021	Deaths 26 July 2020	Deaths 30 April 2021	Deaths per 100 000, 26 July 2020	Deaths per 100 000, 30 April 2021
Moldova	23 034	251 160	735	5 826	18	219.22
Armenia	37 317	216 596	705	4 128	23	139.57
Georgia	1 131	311 457	16	4 130	1	111.01
Ukraine	66 261	2 132 742	1 625	46 281	44	104.27
Azerbaijan	30 050	320 322	417	4 538	4	45.27
Belarus	67 131	359 982	534	2 552	6	26.96

Source: John Hopkins University & Medicine (2021[32]).

Economic activity in the region significantly contracted during the first months of the crisis in 2020. Key economic sectors (extractive, services, tourism, transport) were particularly affected. The collapse in oil prices hit Azerbaijan and Belarus directly but also affected other EaP countries through its impact on trade. Meanwhile, the travel ban led to reduced remittances. All this further exacerbated the socio-economic consequences of the crisis. According to World Bank (2020[33]), the regional economy is forecast to contract by 4.7% in 2021, with recessions in nearly all countries.

Most EaP governments swiftly implemented measures to mitigate the economic impact of COVID-19 on households and businesses. These immediate rescue as well as medium-term recovery packages are significant, totalling about USD 2 billion in Belarus and Ukraine. They also testify to the capacity of the governments to mobilise resources and put in place policies when a crisis hits.

Annex H provides an overview of the main measures the EaP governments put in place to help reduce impacts of the crisis in the energy sector. Highlights of the EaP countries' measures are provided below.

In April 2020, the **Armenian government** prepared 22 recovery packages to address the social and economic consequences of the crisis at the announced amount of AMD 150 billion (USD 305 million). The main support measure in the energy sector targeted consumers of natural gas and electricity who had difficulties paying their utility bills (electricity and gas but also water). The government provided direct budget support to utilities selling natural gas and electricity on behalf of eligible consumers based on conditions specified for the measure.

The **Azerbaijani** government put a total of AZN 2.6 billion (USD 1.5 billion) into its support package. In general, the energy sector is not included in the category of areas affected by the pandemic and needing aid. However, the Government Support Programme "100 kWh of Preferential Light Limit for the Population" provided support to residential users of electricity for April-May 2020.

Belarus has announced a support package of BYN 5 to 6 billion (USD 2 to 2.5 billion). In April 2020, the President of Belarus signed a decree on the reimbursement of part of the costs of works performed in residential buildings and related to improving the efficiency of electric heating and hot water supply. This reimbursement represents 20% of the cost but should not be more than 40 basic units (1 BB – BYR 27) (about USD 495). The subsidy, provided by local budgets, is estimated to benefit about 15 000 consumers annually (USD 6.6 million). The Belarusian government has not yet determined the timeframe for transition to full cost recovery by the population for heat and gas supply services.

In April 2020, the government of **Georgia** announced a recovery package of GEL 3.5 billion (about USD 1.1 billion). To alleviate the impacts of the COVID-19 pandemic, the state budget financed three-month utility bills for households (March, April, May 2020). According to the Georgian National Energy and Water Supply Regulatory Commission, about GEL 150 million (USD 43.5 million) was allocated for this measure. More than 1.2 million electricity customers and more than 670 000 natural gas customers were participating in the subsidy scheme. All consumers eligible for this support could refuse the payments from the state budget. In these three months, more than 9 600 consumers declined to participate in the subsidy scheme as a sign of solidarity. In March 2020, 3 534 consumers declined to join the scheme; in April, another 4 600 consumers also declined.

To support businesses and the economy, the government of **Moldova** put together a support package of LEU 2.5 billion (USD 150 million). It does not envisage specific direct support measures in the energy sector. However, it introduced a regulation banning the disconnection of customers in case of late payment for communal services, including for electricity and heat.

In **Ukraine,** the government committed UAH 65 billion (USD 2.4 billion) in support. In early 2020, It established a special Stabilisation Fund within the general fund of the state budget for the quarantine period (lasting 30 days after the end of the quarantine). It did not identify specific measures for the energy sector as part of the Stabilisation Fund. However, analysis of planned spending before the crisis (January 2020) and after budget amendments (April 2020) shows the government revised budget spending in the energy sector as well. For example, it cut spending on several state support programmes in the coal sector. However, it nearly doubled expenditure on the restructuring of the coal sector. This increased total subsidies to the coal sector by UAH 837 million (USD 30 million).

Most recovery measures in the energy sector are largely concentrated in the electricity sector, where governments and utilities have made commitments to avoid difficulties during the crisis. These include additional assistance with bills or bans on disconnecting customers in arrears. The short-term justification for action is clear. However, for the vitality of these power sectors, temporary measures introduced during the crisis should not grow into longer-lasting subsidy programmes. Recovery support could be more effective when it is aligned with long-term price signals.

References

Center of Public Monitoring and Control of Ukraine (2019), "Monetisation of subsidies: Did the experiment succeed?", 2 September, Center of Public Monitoring and Control, https://naglyad.org/uk/2019/09/02/monetizatsiya-subsidij-eksperiment-vdavsya/. [31]

EITI (2020), "EITI Status of Armenia", webpage, https://eiti.org/armenia (accessed on 5 February 2021). [10]

EITI (2020), "EITI Status of Ukraine", webpage, https://eiti.org/ukraine#eiti-reports-and-other-key-documents (accessed on 5 February 2021). [8]

EITI (2018), "EITI Status of Azerbaijan", webpage, https://eiti.org/azerbaijan (accessed on 4 February 2021). [11]

Ekonomichna Pravda (2018), "The price of imported gas for Ukraine exceeded USD 300", 20 September, Ekonomichna Pravda, https://www.epravda.com.ua/news/2018/09/20/640759/. [15]

Eurostat (2019), "European Neighbourhood Policy: East – Economic Statistics", webpage, https://ec.europa.eu/eurostat/statistics-explained/index.php/European_Neighbourhood_Policy_-_East_-_economic_statistics#General_government_deficit_and_debt (accessed on 30 November 2020). [22]

EY (2018), *EITI National Report of Ukraine 2016*, EY, City, https://eiti.org/files/documents/english_2016_ua_eiti_report.pdf. [9]

Fitch Ratings (2020), "Fitch affirms Azerbaijan's SOCAR at 'BB+'; Outlook stable", 28 January, Rating Action Commentary, Fitch Ratings, https://www.fitchratings.com/research/corporate-finance/fitch-affirms-azerbaijan-socar-at-bb-outlook-stable-28-01-2020. [20]

Fitch Ratings (2020), "Fitch affirms Naftogaz at 'B'; Outlook positive", 2 April, Rating Action Commentary, Fitch Ratings, https://www.fitchratings.com/research/corporate-finance/fitch-affirms-naftogaz-at-b-outlook-positive-02-04-2020. [19]

IEA (2020), *Data and statistics*, database, https://www.iea.org/data-and-statistics/data-tables?country=WORLD (accessed on 14 January 2021). [12]

IEA (2019), *Energy Subsidies - Tracking the impact of Fossil-Fuel Subsidies*, webpage, https://www.iea.org/topics/energy-subsidies (accessed on 12 June 2020). [14]

John Hopkins University & Medicine (2021), "Armenia", *Coronavirus Resource Center*, (database), https://coronavirus.jhu.edu/region/armenia (accessed on 30 April 2021). [32]

Kojima, M. and D. Koplow (2015), "Fossil fuel subsidies: Approaches and valuation", *Policy Research Working Papers*, No. 7220, World Bank Group, Washington, DC, https://openknowledge.worldbank.org/handle/10986/21659. [5]

Miljević, D. (2020), *Investments into the Past. An Analysis of Direct Subsidies to Coal and Lignite Electricity Production in the Energy Community Contracting Parties 2018-2019*, Energy Community, https://energy-community.org/news/Energy-Community-News/2020/12/02.html. [24]

Ministry of Finance of Ukraine (2020), *List of Tax Benefits and Charges (Mandatory Payments) with Estimates of the Revenue Forgone for the Consolidated Budget of Ukraine in 2019 and Forecast for 2020 (Prepared within Budget Supporting Documentation)*, Ministry of Finance of Ukraine, Kyiv, http://w1.c1.rada.gov.ua/pls/zweb2/webproc4_1?pf3511=66853.   [7]

Ministry of Social Policy of Ukraine (2019), "Large-scale monetisation of subsidies has started in Ukraine", 1 March, News, Ministry of Social Policy of Ukraine, Kyiv, https://www.msp.gov.ua/news/16768.html.   [30]

Naftogaz Group (2019), *Annual Report 2019 – On to New Heights*, Naftogaz Group, Kyiv, https://www.naftogaz.com/files/Zvity/Naftogaz_2019_EN.pdf.   [18]

Naftogaz of Ukraine (2016), *Annual Report 2016 – In the Black*, Naftogaz of Ukraine, Kyiv, https://www.naftogaz.com/files/Zvity/Anual_report_eng_170608.pdf.   [17]

Natural Resource Governance Institute (2020), *National Oil Company Database*, (database), https://www.nationaloilcompanydata.org/ (accessed on 30 October 2020).   [21]

NEURC (2016), "Stages of Tariff Changes for Electricity for Household Consumers", webpage, https://www.nerc.gov.ua/?id=19527 (accessed on 1 June 2020).   [16]

OECD (2018), *Inventory of Energy Subsidies in the EU's Eastern Partnership Countries*, Green Finance and Investment, OECD Publishing, Paris, https://dx.doi.org/10.1787/9789264284319-en.   [1]

OECD (2015), *OECD Companion to the Inventory of Support Measures for Fossil Fuels 2015*, OECD Publishing, Paris, https://dx.doi.org/10.1787/9789264239616-en.   [2]

OECD (2013), *Analysing Energy Subsidies in the Countries of Eastern Europe, Caucasus and Central Asia*, OECD Publishing, Paris, https://www.oecd.org/env/outreach/EHS%20report_20%20August%202013_ENG.pdf.   [4]

State Statistics Service of Ukraine (2020), *Data on the Provision of Subsidies to Households in 2019*, State Statistics Service of Ukraine, Kyiv, http://www.ukrstat.gov.ua/express/expr2020/01/05.pdf.   [29]

State Statistics Service of Ukraine (2019), *Data on the Provision of Subsidies to Households in 2018*, State Statistics Service of Ukraine, Kyiv, http://www.ukrstat.gov.ua/.   [28]

State Statistics Service of Ukraine (2019), *Social and Demographic Characteristics of Households of Ukraine in 2019*, State Statistics Service of Ukraine, Kyiv, http://www.ukrstat.gov.ua/druk/publicat/kat_u/2019/zb/07/zb_sdhdu2019.pdf.   [27]

State Statistics Service of Ukraine (2018), *Social and Demographic Characteristics of Households of Ukraine in 2018*, State Statistics Service of Ukraine, Kyiv, http://www.ukrstat.gov.ua/druk/publicat/kat_u/2018/zb/07/zb_sdhdu2018pdf.pdf.   [26]

State Treasury Service of Ukraine (2020), *Reports on the Execution of the State Budget for the Period 2010-2019*, State Treasury Service of Ukraine, Kyiv, https://www.treasury.gov.ua/ua/file-storage/vikonannya-derzhavnogo-byudzhetu.   [6]

Trade Economics (2020), "Azerbaijan Gasoline Prices", *Trading Economics*, (database), https://tradingeconomics.com/azerbaijan/gasoline-prices (accessed on 12 June 2020).   [13]

Voitko, A. (2015), "This year's spending on subsidies 'bypassed' last year's billions", 21 December, Housing News, Chief Expert of Housing and Communal Services of Ukraine, Kyiv, http://statistic.jkg-portal.com.ua/ua/publication/one/vitrati-u-comu-roc-na-subsidji-objshli-minulorchn-na-mljardi-45933. [25]

World Bank (2020), "Economy", *World Bank Open Data*, (database), https://data.worldbank.org/ (accessed on 19 June 2020). [23]

World Bank (2020), *Global Economic Prospects, June 2020*, World Bank, Washington DC, https://www.worldbank.org/en/publication/global-economic-prospects. [33]

WTO (1996), *Agreement on Subsidies and Countervailing Measures*, World Trade Organization, Geneva, https://www.wto.org/english/docs_e/legal_e/24-scm_01_e.htm. [3]

Notes

[1] Armenia, Georgia, Moldova and Ukraine signed the ASCM, while Azerbaijan and Belarus were at different stages of the WTO accession at the time of writing this report.

[2] The price at the border of a good that is imported, which includes international transport costs and tariffs.

[3] The price of a product at the nearest international hub, adjusted for a number of variables such as, among others, the cost of transport, insurance, cost of internal distribution and marketing.

[4] As of 1 January 2021, the Council of Ministers of Ukraine abolished the reduced tariff for electricity for households of UAH 0.9 per kWh for the first 100 kWh consumed and set a fixed price for households at the level of UAH 1.68 per kWh.

[5] In certain cases, it has been difficult to estimate the value of the subsidy for specific fuels because government data are aggregated across several fuels. For example, data on subsidies to crude oil and natural gas in Azerbaijan are bundled together. Similarly, other countries report subsidies to natural gas and electricity as one. Ukraine reports some subsidies as a single number but the support goes to several fuels such as coal, fuel oil and natural gas.

[6] The Ministry of Finance of Armenia does not consider the excise tax exemption on natural gas imports as a subsidy. According to the country's tax legislation, imported natural gas is not subject to an excise tax. For this reason, it is not included in the list of products exempt from excise tax. However, other major fossil fuels in Armenia are all subject to an excise tax. These include lubricating oil, raw oil and oil materials, compressed natural gas, gases produced from oil and other hydro-carbons, petrol and diesel. Unlike other fossil fuels, imported natural gas is exempt from an excise tax. This gives rise to a tax expenditure, which is why the study includes this exemption as a subsidy.

3 Main energy pricing and energy taxation policies in the Eastern Partner countries

This chapter focuses on the main energy pricing and energy taxation policies in the six European Union's Eastern Partner (EaP) countries (Armenia, Azerbaijan, Belarus, Georgia, Republic of Moldova and Ukraine) with direct or indirect impact on the evolution of fossil-fuel subsidies. It also reviews the main macroeconomic trends that characterise the economies of these countries in light of the most recent developments caused by the COVID-19 crisis. Finally, it discusses the energy mix and energy productivity of the EaP economies, as well as recent changes in the energy pricing and taxation policies and their significance for the reforms of fossil-fuel subsidies.

Macroeconomic trends

The European Union's Eastern Partner (EaP) countries (Armenia, Azerbaijan, Belarus, Georgia, Republic of Moldova and Ukraine) differ in the size of their population and economy, as well as level of economic development.1 Ukraine is by far the largest of the six economies with 2018 gross domestic product (GDP) at USD 130.8 billion. It is followed by Belarus and Azerbaijan, with GDP at USD 59.7 billion and USD 46.9 billion, respectively. Georgia, Armenia and the Republic of Moldova (hereafter "Moldova") are the smallest economies (Table 3.1). In 2018, however, Belarus and Azerbaijan had the highest GDP per capita – approximately USD 20 000 and USD 18 000 (current international USD, purchasing power parity – PPP), respectively (Table 3.1). Armenia and Georgia had the highest GDP growth rate in 2018.

The population of the EaP countries was around 73.4 million people in 2018. All EaP countries were affected by the coronavirus pandemic in 2020. At the time of the writing of this report, they were revising their short-term macroeconomic forecasts and budget spending.

Table 3.1. Key economic indicators of EaP countries in 2018

	Population, million	GDP growth rate, percentage	GDP, billion current USD
Armenia	3.0	5.2	12.4
Azerbaijan	9.9	1.5	46.9*
Belarus	9.5	3.1	59.7
Georgia	3.7	4.8	17.6
Moldova	2.7	4.3	11.4
Ukraine	44.6	3.3	130.8

Note: *According to national statistics (as communicated by the Ministry of Economy of Azerbaijan), GDP in Azerbaijan in 2018 amounted to USD 47.1 billion.
Source: World Bank (2020[1]).

To ensure cross-country comparisons, this chapter relies on *World Bank Open Data* and other sources of international statistics. Exchange rates of the national currencies in the six countries have been volatile over 1991-2019. National currencies of most countries in the region depreciated against the US dollar in 2015, shrinking their GDP in dollar terms even when the economy grew in real terms (Annex A).

Despite many differences, the six countries share several common strengths, including a highly educated workforce and the continued opening of their economies to trade and investment opportunities. Armenia, Georgia, Moldova and Ukraine are World Trade Organization (WTO) members, while Azerbaijan and Belarus are negotiating their accession. As of March 2017, all six EaP countries had signed the European Union (EU)-led Energy Charter Treaty to support energy trade and investment.[2] They all later ratified it, except for Belarus, which applied the treaty provisionally (IEC, n.d.[2]). Armenia and Belarus are also members of the Eurasian Economic Union (EAEU)[3] and its Customs Union, which provides for further integration of the countries' energy systems.

Figure 3.1. GDP per capita, purchasing power parity, current international USD

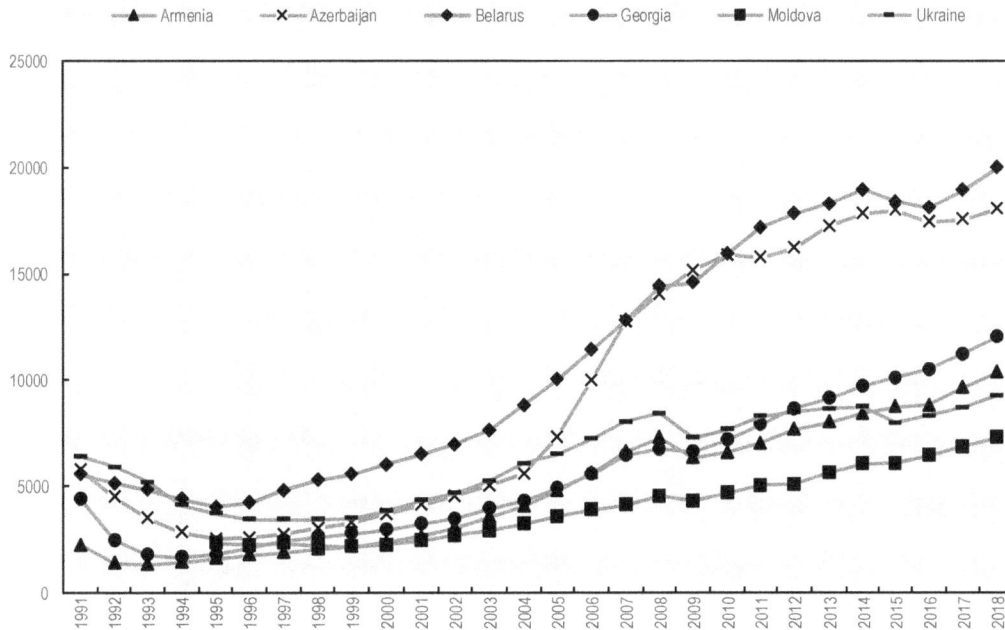

Source: World Bank (2020[1]).

The EaP countries share a common macroeconomic pattern. GDP decreased sharply in the years after the collapse of the Soviet Union in 1991. This was followed by restructuring and modernisation of their economies and restoration of economic growth in the late 1990s and 2000s. Overall, from 1991 to 2018, the six EaP economies have all grown in real terms (World Bank, 2020[1]). All EaP countries developed a large service sector that contributed to over third of the value-added in each country (Figure 3.2). Meanwhile, personal remittances constitute a considerable share of the GDP – more than 10% in most countries except Azerbaijan and Belarus (Figure 3.2).

Figure 3.2. Structure of the economy and personal remittances received, share of GDP, 2018

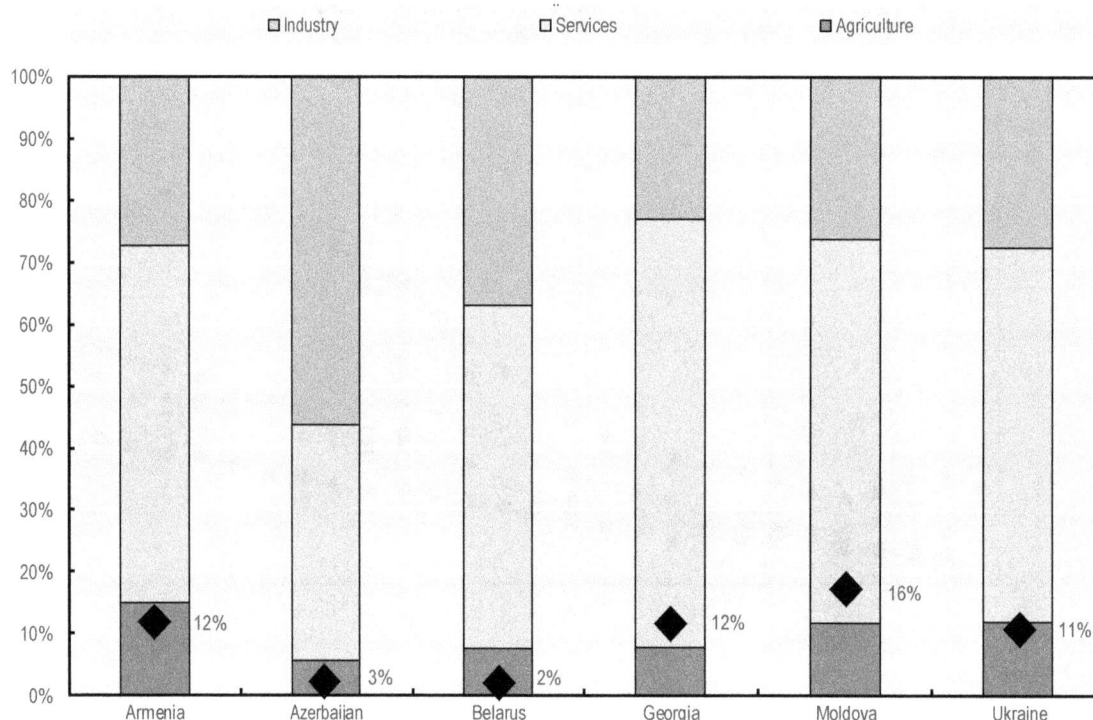

Note: In this figure, remittances as a share of GDP are indicated by the black diamond.
Source: World Bank (2020[1]).

The six countries' economic performance is sensitive to fluctuations in international commodity markets[4] and regional linkages. All EaP countries experience fiscal pressures: central budget deficits ranged from 0.3% in Azerbaijan to 1.9% in Ukraine. Meanwhile, Belarus was the only country with a budgetary surplus (4%) in 2018 (Eurostat, 2019[3]).

The COVID-19 crisis significantly aggravated the economic performance of the EaP countries in 2020. The health crisis has triggered an economic crisis, which is turning into a global recession. The pandemic has brought about a collapse of commodity prices, tourism, remittances and exports, as well as supply chain disruptions and financial market confusion. COVID-19 has exposed countries' vulnerabilities and lack of preparedness to fight major crises.

According to the International Monetary Fund (IMF, 2021[4]), real economic growth in the EaP region contracted on average by 5.1% in 2020. Armenia and Moldova experienced the deepest economic downturn (-7.8% and -7.5%, respectively), followed by Georgia (-6.1%). Azerbaijan and Ukraine did somewhat "better" (-4.3% and -4.2%, respectively). Real economic growth in Belarus contracted year-on-year in 2020 by 0.9%. Growth in the region is forecast to rebound in 2021, as global commodity prices gradually recover, trade strengthens and domestic demand improves. However, many uncertainties remain.

Energy mix and energy productivity

In the political and economic transition from central planning to market orientation, the energy systems of the EaP countries have undergone several waves of reforms and restructuring. These changes, still in progress, are subject to several key drivers.

Except for Azerbaijan, the EaP countries are net energy importers (Figure 3.3). Thus, energy security is a major issue for most countries in the region. The Russian Federation (hereafter "Russia"), Azerbaijan and, to a certain extent, the Central Asian states (such as Kazakhstan, Turkmenistan) are key energy suppliers. Increasingly, the EaP countries are set to leverage their strategic position. On the one hand, Russia and Central Asia export energy. On the other, the European Union and the People's Republic of China are major markets for natural gas and oil.

Figure 3.3. Total energy supply of EaP countries in 2017, mtoe

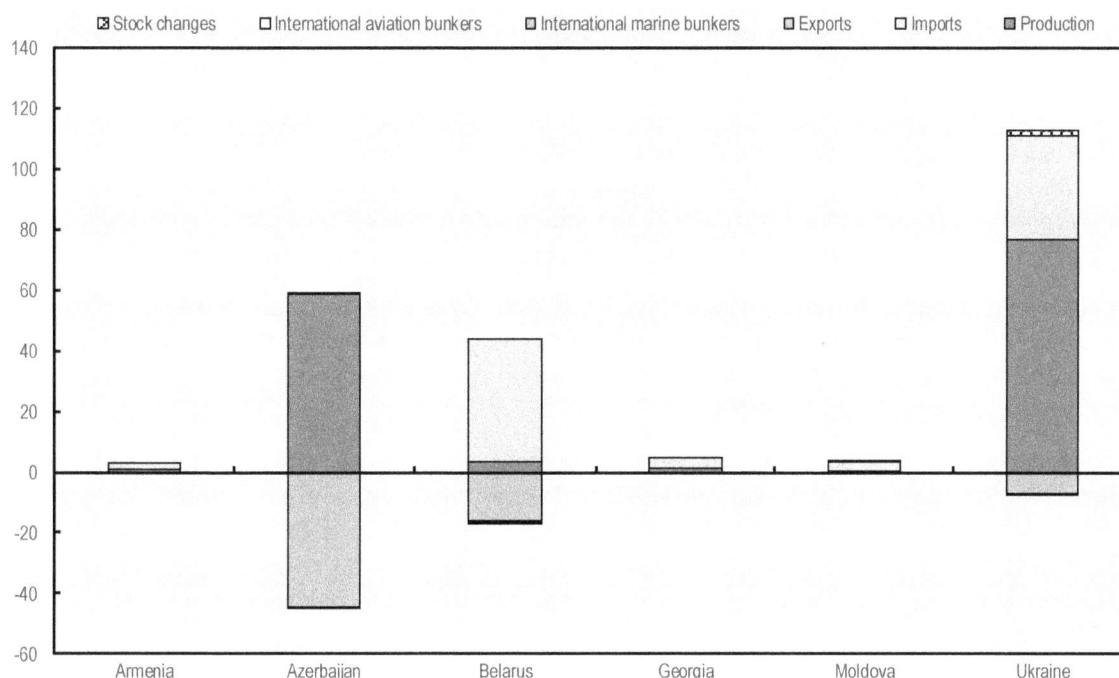

Note: mtoe – million tonnes of oil equivalent.
Source: IEA (2020[5]).

Fossil fuels continue to dominate the region's energy sector. Except for Ukraine, the share of natural gas in the total primary energy supply has increased in the region at the expense of fuel oil. There are several drivers behind this trend. For example, Azerbaijan has increased its own production of natural gas. Meanwhile, Belarus, Armenia, Moldova and to a certain extent Georgia, have access to affordable imports of natural gas, mainly from Russia. These countries also introduced market pricing for oil products following the collapse of the Soviet Union. Box 3.1 provides more details on the energy mix in individual EaP countries.

Box 3.1. Energy mix in EaP countries

Armenia has no domestic resources of fossil fuels. It relies on domestically generated electricity and imported natural gas to meet most of its energy consumption needs. Imported natural gas dominates the total energy supply (TES) in Armenia. It accounts for 61% of Armenia's TES and 85% of the fossil-fuel (including jet fuel) consumption in 2017.

Azerbaijan is rich in deposits of oil and natural gas and has, over the last decade, become a major energy producer. As of 2019, total proven reserves of oil and natural gas amount to 7 000 million barrels and 2.1 trillion cubic metres, respectively. Oil production stood at 39.2 million tonnes[5] in 2018, roughly 24% less than the peak of 51.3 million tonnes in 2010. In 2017, natural gas and oil constituted 64% and 35% of TES, respectively.

Belarus is a net energy importer whose domestic sources covered only 15% of TES. The country relies heavily on imported natural gas and oil for power production (97% gas-fired generation). Its export-oriented refining and petrochemical industry exported about 13 million tonnes of oil equivalent (mtoe) of oil products in 2017. This was an important source of hard currency for the country.

Georgia is a net importer of energy. It relies heavily on natural gas imports from Azerbaijan, and various imports of oil products and coal. The country's domestic energy production centres around hydropower, biomass and some coal. In 2017, natural gas and oil accounted for 41% and 30% of TES, respectively, while the share of hydropower was 16%.

Moldova depends highly on energy imports, as domestic production (mostly biofuels and waste) accounted for approximately 21% of supply in 2017. Moldova imports natural gas, oil products, coal and electricity and the former two energy carriers constituted 51% and 23% of TES, respectively. Moldova began construction of the Ungheni-Chișinău pipeline (120 km) in 2018 to diversify gas supplies from Russia and to connect with the European gas market. Completion is planned for 2021 at a cost of EUR 70-90 million.

In 2017, domestic production covered 66% of TES in **Ukraine** with the largest shares from nuclear (22.4 mtoe), natural gas (15.5 mtoe) and coal (13.7 mtoe). In the same year, power plants and combined heat and power (CHP) plants used roughly a third of energy supply to generate 156 terawatt hours (TWh) of electricity. Nuclear and coal-fired power plants contributed 54% and 32% to the electricity generation mix, respectively.

Source: Based on IEA (2020[5]) data.

Renewable energy plays a negligible role in the region, except for significant hydropower generation in Georgia. Belarus, Ukraine and Moldova also produce biomass and biofuels for energy use, while Armenia and Ukraine generate nuclear power. Belarus is completing the construction of its first nuclear power plant (the launch of the first unit was postponed several times).

The transition from a centrally planned to market economy has coincided with lack of revenue and capital for infrastructure maintenance and modernisation and the need for new funding sources. The assets built in Soviet times are still the backbone of the energy infrastructure in the EaP countries. As a result, the region's economies are still highly energy-intensive. Figure 3.4 shows that each of the EaP countries produced more dollars of GDP in 2017 than in 1990 per unit of energy consumed.

Some productivity gains have been made, but performance has been uneven across the EaP countries. Azerbaijan is in a unique position as an energy exporter. Since 1990, Armenia has led the region with a more than fivefold improvement of energy productivity of GDP. Meanwhile, Ukraine has only improved its energy productivity by 1.8-times, only slightly more than half the progress made by Belarus.

Figure 3.4. Energy productivity in EaP countries, GDP per unit of energy use, constant 2011 PPP USD per kg of oil equivalent

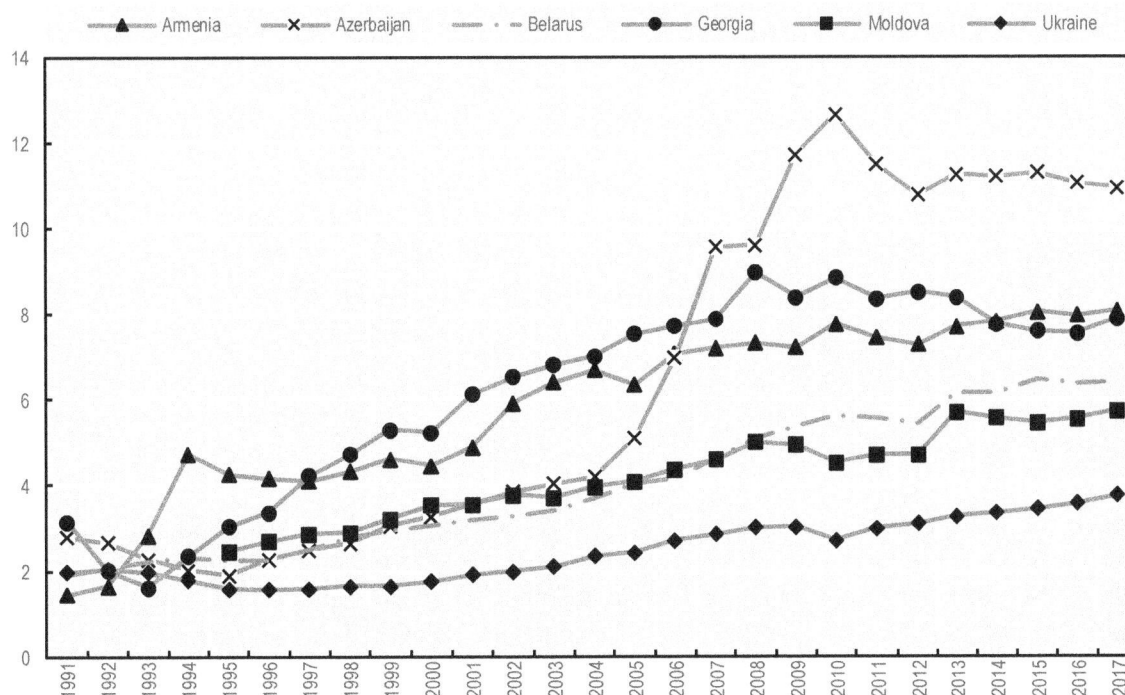

Source: Estimated indicator based on World Bank (2020[1]) and IEA (2020[5]).

Key energy pricing policies

Energy pricing is highly regulated in the EaP countries. The most commonly used term for an energy pricing policy in the region is "tariff regulation". Energy price liberalisation remains socially and politically sensitive because price regulation is still considered important to protect socially vulnerable households, support industrial competitiveness and restrain inflation. Some countries have abandoned "blanket" subsidies provided through low tariffs for more targeted support schemes.

Table 3.2 provides an overview of the key characteristics of energy pricing policies in each country.

Table 3.2. Key characteristics of energy pricing policies in EaP countries as of end 2019

	Armenia	Azerbaijan	Belarus	Georgia	Moldova	Ukraine
Price-setting authority	Public Services Regulatory Commission	Tariff Council	The Council of Ministers, Ministry for Anti-Monopoly Regulation and Trade	Georgian National Energy and Water Supply Regulatory Commission	National Energy Regulatory Agency	National Energy and Utilities Regulatory Commission, Cabinet of Ministers of Ukraine
Natural gas	Regulated prices	Regulated prices	Regulated prices, cross-subsidies	Mostly regulated prices, elements of both cross-subsidies and deregulation	Regulated prices	Regulated prices for households, deregulated prices for industry
Electricity						Regulated prices, cross-subsidies
Heat	n.a.			n.a.		Regulated prices
Liquid petroleum products	Deregulated prices		Regulated prices	Deregulated prices		
Coal and other solid fuels						

Note:* n.a. – Not applicable.
Source: Adopted and updated from from OECD (2018[6]).

Except for Belarus, where energy prices for the population are set by the Council of Ministers and for legal entities - by the Ministry for Anti-Monopoly Regulation and Trade (except for heat generated by entities outside of the "Belenergo" State Production Association), all other EaP countries have set up dedicated bodies for energy tariff-setting. The degree of independence enjoyed by these new institutions varies across countries and periods between the waves of reforms. Interference from governments and state-owned energy companies in tariff setting has been quite common. Consequently, the recovery of costs in the energy sector continues to be lower than it could be.

The natural gas, heat and electricity sectors remain subject to price regulation in all EaP countries, for consumers as well as often for producers. Different groups of consumers and producers normally have different tariffs. Formally, price-setting methodologies for most energy types are publicly available and, at least in theory, based on the "cost-plus" methodology. However, the cost-recovery concept is often limited to operational costs. It is insufficient to recover long-run investment and modernisation expenditure. The market for liquid petroleum products is the most deregulated segment in the region; only Azerbaijan and Belarus regulate prices in this sector.

Pricing policies, including methodologies, tariff structures and regulations, continue to evolve in the EaP region. For example, the Georgian National Energy and Water Supply Regulatory Commission, in line with international standards in electricity and gas sectors, has abandoned tariff setting based on memoranda. Its tariff regulation is completely subject to the Commission's normative acts (tariff methodologies).

In 2018, Moldova decreased electricity and natural gas tariffs by 10% and 20%, respectively, in response to currency appreciation; tariffs for heating remain unchanged.

On 2 December 2013, the Tariff Council of Azerbaijan announced an increase of state-regulated price ceilings for gasoline, diesel and natural gas for industrial facilities. This resulted in price increases for petroleum products of about 27-33% and almost 50% for natural gas. This decision – the first adjustment since 2007 – was apparently taken to compensate for the loss in government revenue due to the decline in oil production[6] (RFE/RL's Azerbaijani Service, 2013[7]). In previous years, Tariff Council proposals for tariff increases were cancelled following interventions from the Azerbaijani Presidency.

The government of Ukraine implemented a substantial increase of utility tariffs in 2014-17 and further reformed pricing policies. This helped reduce the deficits of utility providers and consequently cut or eliminated various government compensation schemes. Rather than keeping low tariffs for all households for social and political reasons, the government has also gradually reformed its social support programmes to target eligible low-income households (Box 2.3).

Compared to the first EaP Inventory (OECD, 2018[6]) relatively little has changed in the energy pricing policies in the EaP countries. Gas price reform lies at the heart of the energy sector and fossil-fuel subsidy reforms in the region. Among the EaP countries, Ukraine has implemented some of the most significant pricing reforms in recent years. These include, among others, increasing tariffs for the population to levels closer to cost recovery of gas, electricity and heat supply; eliminating regulated tariffs for industrial users and recently natural gas tariffs for households;[7] and strengthening targeted social support programmes for poor people. The real challenge for the country is to ensure that new governments do not abandon these reforms but rather further improve them.

The COVID-19 crisis and lower international energy prices coupled with reduced energy demand open up yet another window of opportunity for the countries in the region. They may wish to re-assess their energy pricing policies, depoliticise them (e.g. introduce price adjustment formulae) and consider adequate measures to protect the vulnerable segments of the population.

Main taxation policies

In the past two decades, the EaP countries have made efforts to reform their fiscal systems to reduce administrative barriers, simplify taxation and thus increase collection of tax revenue. Baseline taxation in all EaP countries includes value-added tax (VAT), corporate profit tax, individual income tax, property tax, land tax and a single tax for small businesses – all codified at the national level and passed into law.

Most countries also charge additional local taxes, a road tax on vehicles and fees for environmental pollution. Belarus applies a lowering 0.27 coefficient to environmental tax rates on certain emissions. The rate applies on emissions generated from fossil-fuel combustion by power plants that provide electricity and heat for households and social service institutions in health care, tourism and sports, education and culture (National Assembly of the Republic of Belarus, 2002[8]).

In the extractive sector, the three countries with scalable production of fossil fuels – Azerbaijan, Belarus and Ukraine – charge a mining tax on their production, which is differentiated by type of deposit. Azerbaijan and Georgia also have special taxation regimes for large-scale energy projects implemented by foreign investors such as oil and gas extraction and pipelines. These operate under the so-called Production Sharing Agreements and Host Government Agreements.

The import and export of energy products are subject to customs duties. Consumption of petrol and diesel in all EaP countries is also subject to an excise tax. Liquefied petroleum gas (LPG) and compressed natural gas (CNG) are also excise goods in most EaP countries (Table 3.3). To encourage use of LPG and CNG, many EU countries charge a lower excise rate for these fuels than for petrol or diesel. Among the EaP countries, only Armenia has applied this practice.

Governments determine excise tax rates. They revise the rates relatively often to reflect energy price fluctuations on international markets and to raise sufficient funds for national budgets. Azerbaijan, Belarus and Ukraine differentiate excise tax rates depending on the grade of petrol and diesel. For their part, Armenia, Georgia and Moldova have single excise tax rates for both petrol and diesel. Only Ukraine levies an excise tax on electricity. Natural gas and thermal energy are not subject to excise taxes in the EaP countries.

Excise fuel taxes are often seen as an implicit carbon price. They are similar to carbon prices in that the tax liability increases proportionally to fossil-fuel use. However, this is not a consistent carbon price across all fuels; the excise tax is applied only to some fuels. Reforming fuel excise taxes to better align with the climate costs of fuel use would be administratively straightforward (OECD, 2021[9]).

VAT and excise taxes form part of the end price for energy goods. Thus, they exist within the wider context of energy price regulation in the EaP countries (see section on Key energy pricing policies). The EaP governments use tax exemptions and adjustments in excise tax rates as tools to adjust consumer energy prices. For example, Armenia had a VAT exemption for diesel imports until the end of 2017. Additionally, tax breaks are used to promote investment in the energy sector in the region (see Chapter 2, section on Budget transfers and revenue foregone).

No EaP country except Ukraine has an explicit carbon tax. Ukraine introduced a carbon price with the approval of the new Tax Code in 2010. The carbon tax on stationary sources of pollution had initially a low rate, but it was increased to UAH 10/tCO_2 (USD 0.4/tCO_2) in 2019 (Parliament of Ukraine, 2010[10]). In April 2021, the Ministry of Finance submitted to Parliament a draft law informally known as the "Resources Law" (Parliament of Ukraine, 2021[11]). Among other things, this draft law envisages an increase of the carbon tax rate from UAH 10/tCO_2 to UAH 30/tCO_2 (USD 1.08/tCO_2) (Interfax-Ukraine, 2021[12]).

The Ukrainian government understands that a carbon tax of USD 1 or below will have little impact on energy prices. As the carbon tax rate in Ukraine is still low relative to fossil-fuel prices and compared to the cost of many CO_2 reduction technologies, it primarily fulfils a fiscal function. However, despite its low rate, the tax is gaining in significance across local businesses. It also has the potential to mobilise additional resources that could be allocated to support new green investments in the country.

Armenia is the only other country in the region that has expressed interest in a carbon tax. The government of Armenia committed to a carbon tax in its Nationally Determined Contribution, which was prepared for the Paris Summit on Climate Change in 2015. However, the document has no specific timing for introducing such a tax. Both Armenia and Ukraine are considering the possibility to use the carbon tax revenue to finance climate change mitigation and adaptation projects.

OECD countries commonly use EUR 30 per tonne of CO_2 as their benchmark carbon rate. This is the low-end estimate for the carbon price needed in the near term for consistency with the net-zero CO_2 emission targets (OECD, 2021[9]). This price is expected to rise to EUR 120 in the 2030s. Supporting such a trajectory, in May 2021, the EU carbon price went above EUR 50 per tonne of CO_2 for the first time, reflecting market expectations for policy triggers to incentivise investments in innovative clean technologies.

The impacts of carbon pricing on energy prices are of particular concern as they affect the distributional burden on households and industries. A recent study of several countries (IMF/OECD, 2021[13]) estimates that increasing the carbon tax up to the level of USD 50 per tonne of CO_2 in 2030 will significantly increase their electricity prices. For example, such a tax increase would likely raise electricity prices in Indonesia by 75%, in Russia by 65%, in South Africa by 61%, in Turkey by 60% and in Mexico by 58%.

The impact on electricity prices will depend on the countries' mix of power generation fuels. The impact of carbon price on coal (given its high carbon intensity) and gas will be considerable but will be smaller on pump prices for motor fuels. Therefore, the implications of a higher carbon tax to encourage decarbonisation of the economy should be well understood and accompanied by incentives to ensure affordable access to cleaner alternatives.

Table 3.3. VAT and excise tax rates on energy consumption in EaP countries

	Armenia	Azerbaijan	Belarus	Georgia	Moldova	Ukraine
Petrol						
VAT rate	20%	18%	20%	18%	20%	20%
Excise rate	Not differentiated by grade	Differentiated by grade	Differentiated by grade	Not differentiated by grade	Not differentiated by grade	Differentiated by grade
Diesel						
VAT rate	20%	18%	20%	18%	20%	20%
Excise rate	Not differentiated by grade	Differentiated by grade	Differentiated by grade	Not differentiated by grade	Not differentiated by grade	Differentiated by grade
CNG						
VAT rate	20%	18%	20%	18%	20%	20%
Excise rate	Yes	Yes	Yes (if used as motor fuel)	Yes	No	Yes
LPG						
VAT rate	20%	18%	20%	18%	8% for households only, 20% for other users	20%
Excise rate	Yes	Yes	Yes (if used as motor fuel)	Yes	Yes	Yes (exemption on sales for households at specialised auctions)
Natural gas						
VAT rate	20%	18%	20%	18%, VAT exemption for natural gas imported for thermal power stations	8% for households only, 20% for other users	20%
Electricity						
VAT rate	20%	18%	20%	18%	0% for households, 20% for other users	20%
Excise rate	No	No	No	No	No	3.2%
Heat						
VAT rate	20%	18%	20%	18%	0% for households, 20% for other users	20%

Source: Adopted and updated from OECD (2018[6]).

The taxation regime in the energy sector in the EaP region has not changed much since the analysis of the first Inventory covering 2010-15. Except for Ukraine, the EaP countries do not use carbon pricing. Yet carbon pricing provides across-the-board incentives for firms and households to reduce carbon-intensive energy use and shift to cleaner fuels. It also provides the essential price signal for mobilising private investment in clean technologies while raising government revenue (IMF/OECD, 2021[13]). In this context, Ukraine's experience will provide valuable lessons. However, before introducing such a tax, the EaP governments need to understand its implications on energy prices in their countries.

The recovery packages related to COVID-19 provide an opportunity to reset countries' economies in a greener, more resilient and inclusive way. The EaP governments should use this opportunity to ensure these packages reflect their green and climate ambitions. Fossil-fuel subsidy reform, including energy pricing and taxation, offers key policy measures to support green economic development. Such measures maintain climate commitments while generating revenue to finance pressing social needs.

References

Eurostat (2019), "European Neighbourhood Policy: East – Economic Statistics", webpage, https://ec.europa.eu/eurostat/statistics-explained/index.php/European_Neighbourhood_Policy_-_East_-_economic_statistics#General_government_deficit_and_debt (accessed on 30 November 2020). [3]

IEA (2020), "Energy balances", *Data and Statistics*, (database), https://www.iea.org/data-and-statistics/data-tables?country=WORLD (accessed on 13 May 2020). [5]

IEC (n.d.), *The Energy Charter Treaty*, International Energy Charter, Brussels, https://www.energycharter.org/process/energy-charter-treaty-1994/energy-charter-treaty/. [2]

IMF (2021), *World Economic Outlook*, (database), https://www.imf.org/en/Publications/WEO/weo-database/2021/April/select-country-group (accessed on 14 May 2021). [4]

IMF/OECD (2021), *Tax Policy and Climate Change: IMF/OECD Report for the G20 Finance Ministers and Central Bank Governors, April 2021, Italy*, https://www.oecd.org/tax/tax-policy/imf-oecd-g20-report-tax-policy-and-climate-change.htm. [13]

Interfax-Ukraine (2021), "Ministry of Finance proposes a three-step increase of the CO2 tax rate and a ten-time increase of the water discharge rate over a period of eight years", 22 April, Interfax, Ukraine News Agency, Kyiv, https://interfax.com.ua/news/economic/739371.html. [12]

National Assembly of the Republic of Belarus (2002), *Tax Code of the Republic of Belarus No. 166-3 of 19 December 2002 (with Amendments of 2009) and No. 71-3 of 29 December 2009*, National Assembly of the Republic of Belarus, Minsk, https://etalonline.by/document/?regnum=Hk0200166, https://etalonline.by/document/?regnum=Hk0900071. [8]

OECD (2021), *Taxing Energy Use for Sustainable Development: Opportunities for Energy Tax and Subsidy Reform in Selected Developing and Emerging Economies*, OECD, Paris, https://www.oecd.org/tax/tax-policy/taxing-energy-use-for-sustainable-development.htm. [9]

OECD (2018), *Inventory of Energy Subsidies in the EU's Eastern Partnership Countries*, Green Finance and Investment, OECD Publishing, Paris, https://doi.org/10.1787/9789264284319-en. [6]

Parliament of Ukraine (2021), *Draft Law on Amendments to the Tax Code of Ukraine and Certain Legislative Acts of Ukraine to Ensure Balance of Budget Revenues*, https://w1.c1.rada.gov.ua/pls/zweb2/webproc4_1?pf3511=72106. [11]

Parliament of Ukraine (2010), *Tax Code of Ukraine No. 2 755-VI of 2 December 2010 (with Amendments)*, Parliament of Ukraine, Kyiv, https://zakon.rada.gov.ua/laws/show/2755-17#Text. [10]

RFE/RL's Azerbaijani Service (2013), "Azerbaijani prices for gasoline, natural gas rise sharply", 3 December, RadioFreeEurope/RadioLiberty, https://www.rferl.org/a/azerbaijan-raises-gas-prices/25188225.html. [7]

World Bank (2020), *Economy*, (database), https://data.worldbank.org/ (accessed on 23 June 2020).

Notes

[1] Data from international sources are used throughout this chapter to ensure accurate cross-country comparisons.

[2] The Energy Charter Treaty establishes a framework for international co-operation between the European countries and other industrialised counties. This aims to develop the energy potential of Central and Eastern European countries and ensure security of energy supply for the European Union. To that end, countries would operate more open and competitive energy markets, while respecting the principles of sustainable development and sovereignty over energy resources. Key provisions concern protection of investment, trade in energy materials, and products, transit and dispute settlement.

[3] The Eurasian Economic Union (EAEU) is a free trade agreement that came into being in 2015 to increase economic cooperation and raise the standard of living of its members. Member countries include Russia, Armenia, Belarus, Kazakhstan, and Kyrgyzstan. Unlike the European Union, the EAEU does not share a common currency.

[4] Especially in the case of Azerbaijan, the only exporter of energy commodities in the region or in the case of Armenia where mineral exports make up a significant share of the country's exports.

[5] According to national statistics from the Ministry of Economy of Azerbaijan, oil production in Azerbaijan in 2018 was 38.8 million tonnes.

[6] Tariff Council regulation on monopolistic entities (including the areas mentioned in the report) is carried out in accordance with the "Rules for Ensuring State Supervision over the Formation and Application of Tariffs Subject to State Regulation" approved by the Cabinet of Ministers Resolution No. 247, dated 30 December 2005. Prices of oil products (excluding petrol, diesel and bitumen) are no longer regulated by the state. This is in accordance with Resolution No. 1 of the Cabinet of Ministers of Azerbaijan, dated 4 January 2021, on "Amendments to the "List of Goods (Works, Services) whose Prices (Tariffs) are Subject to State Regulation" approved by Cabinet of Ministers Resolution No. 178, dated 28 September 2005.

[7] As of 1 August 2020, the retail price of natural gas for households has been fully liberalised. However, the government of Ukraine has capped the gas price for households at UAH 6.99 per 1 cubic metre (including VAT and transportation fees) over the period of the quarantine due to the COVID-19 pandemic.

Annex A. Currency exchange rates

Table A A.1. Currency exchange rates, National currency per USD

Country	Currency	2010	2011	2012	2013	2014	2015	2016	2017	2018	2019
Armenia	AMD	373.66	372.50	401.76	409.63	415.92	477.92	480.49	482.72	482.99	480.42
Azerbaijan	AZN	0.80	0.79	0.79	0.78	0.78	1.02	1.60	1.72	1.70	1.70
Belarus[1]	BYN	2 978.51	4 974.63	8 336.90	8 880.05	1 0224.10	1 5925.99	1.99	1.93	2.04	2.20
Georgia	GEL	1.78	1.69	1.65	1.66	1.77	2.27	2.37	2.51	2.53	2.87
Moldova	MDL	12.37	11.74	12.11	12.59	14.04	18.82	19.92	18.50	16.80	17.49
Ukraine	UAH	7.94	7.97	7.99	7.99	11.89	21.84	25.55	26.60	27.20	24.74

Note: Although Belarus undertook currency redenomination in 2016 (National Bank of the Republic of Belarus, 2015[1]), exchange rates were not adjusted for 2010-15. Such an adjustment would have implied dividing the respective exchange rates by 10 000, which would have distorted USD subsidy values for the period. To avoid such distortions, the actual unadjusted exchange rate for Belarus for the period before redenomination was used. Currency redenomination means that subsidy values in BYN drop by 10 000 times but time series in USD remain consistent and comparable.
Source: National Accounts and (World Bank, 2020[2])

References

National Bank of the Republic of Belarus (2015), "On redenomination of the Belarusian Ruble since July 1, 2016", 5 November, Press Release, National Bank of the Republic of Belarus, Minsk, https://www.nbrb.by/engl/news/4565. [1]

World Bank (2020), "Economy", World Bank Open Data, (database), https://data.worldbank.org/ (accessed on 29 May 2020). [2]

Annex B. Armenia FFSs

Table A B.1. Fossil-fuel subsidies in Armenia, AMD million

Programme	Mechanism of support	Indicator	Fuel	2010	2011	2012	2013	2014	2015	2016	2017	2018	2019
Compensation to Electric Networks of Armenia for supplying electricity to households and small business at regulated tariff	direct transfer	CSE	electricity	n.a.	n.a.	n.a.	n.a.	n.a.	1 208	688	n.a.	n.a.	n.a.
Compensation to Gazprom-Armenia for natural gas supplied to low-income households	direct transfer	CSE	natural gas	n.a.	544	516	1 053	646	n.a.	n.a.	n.a.	n.a.	n.a.
Partial compensation of electricity and gas consumption costs for border communities	direct transfer	CSE	electricity, natural gas	n.a.	n.a.	n.a.	n.a.	n.a.	928	766	603	532	460
VAT exemption of imported diesel	tax expenditure	CSE	diesel	6 755	8 932	10 919	10 585	10 932	7 613	6 494	8 519	n.a.	n.a.
Excise tax exemption of imported natural gas	tax expenditure	CSE	natural gas	1 126	1 448	1 719	1 653	1 716	1 660	1 625	1 787	1 779	1 880
Excise tax exemption of compressed natural gas	tax expenditure	CSE	natural gas	2 651	3 018	3 482	3 790	4 013	4 037	1 298	n.a.	n.a.	n.a.
Total direct transfers				n.a.	544	516	1 053	646	2 136	1 453	603	532	460
Total tax expenditure				10 533	13 399	16 120	16 028	16 660	13 309	9 416	10 306	1 779	1 880
Total				10 533	13 942	16 636	17 081	17 306	15 445	10 870	10 909	2 310	2 340
Total, OECD (2018) report				-	13 943	16 636	17 081	17 306	17 688	-	-	-	-

Notes:

a. n.a.: not applicable, -: not available.

b. Where the subsidy is provided to more than one sector or fuel, its value in the country table may be somewhat different from the value reported in the OECD Inventory database due to disaggregation across sectors (see Annex I for further explanation). Values of electricity subsidies as reported in the country tables and the online database may also differ. Any difference has occurred because the non-fossil fuel component in electricity generation, as well as in imported electricity, has been subtracted from the electricity subsidy value for the purposes of the OECD database.

c. Reported values of budget transfers to Electric Networks of Armenia were adjusted (multiplied by shares of gas-based generation – 0.35 and 0.36 in 2015 and 2016, respectively) to take into account only the fossil-fuel share of the subsidy, based on the IEA (2020[1]) Energy Balances data.

Source: Authors' compilations and calculations based on data collected for OECD (2020[2]) and previous estimates of fossil-fuel subsidies in the EaP countries published in the OECD (2018[3]) report.

References

IEA (2020), "Data and statistics", *Energy Balances Statistics*, (database), https://www.iea.org/data-and-statistics/data-tables?country=WORLD (accessed on 14 January 2021). [1]

OECD (2020), "OECD-IEA Analysis of Fossil Fuels Support", webpage, http://www.oecd.org/fossil-fuels/publication/ (accessed on 20 May 2020). [2]

OECD (2018), *Inventory of Energy Subsidies in the EU's Eastern Partnership Countries*, Green Finance and Investment, OECD Publishing, Paris, https://doi.org/10.1787/9789264284319-en. [3]

Annex C. Azerbaijan FFSs

Table A C.1. Fossil-fuel subsidies in Azerbaijan, AZN million

Programme	Mechanism of support	Indicator	Fuel	2010	2011	2012	2013	2014	2015	2016	2017	2018	2019
State budget transfer to Azerenerji to cover accumulated losses and debts	direct transfer	CSE	natural gas	72	180	142	72	38	235	115	0.1	300	-
State budget transfers to Azeristilik to cover deficits due to providing services below costs	direct transfer	CSE	natural gas	n.a.	20	-	21	-	23	-	-	33	17
State budget transfers to SOCAR to cover losses of AzerGas	direct transfer	PSE	crude oil, natural gas	n.a.	n.a.	n.a.	n.a.	n.a.	n.a.	n.a.	n.a.	963	1 071
Financial transfers from SOFAZ to energy projects	direct transfer	PSE	crude oil, natural gas	n.a.	n.a.	n.a.	n.a.	n.a.	n.a.	1 823	-	-	-
State budget transfers to cover the utility expenditure of internally displaced persons	direct transfer	CSE	electricity	n.a.	196	-	213	-	228	-	n.a.	248	267
State budget transfers to meet the needs of farmers in diesel and engine lubricants	direct transfer	CSE	diesel, lubricants	-	-	-	-	-	-	-	-	-	-
VAT exemptions under Production Sharing Agreements	tax expenditure	PSE	crude oil, natural gas	-	-	-	-	-	-	-	-	-	-
Customs duties exemptions under Production Sharing Agreements	tax expenditure	PSE	crude oil, natural gas	-	-	-	-	-	-	-	-	-	-
VAT exemptions under Host Government Agreements	tax expenditure	PSE	crude oil, natural gas	-	-	-	-	-	-	-	-	-	-
Customs duties exemptions under Host Government Agreements	tax expenditure	PSE	crude oil, natural gas	-	-	-	-	-	-	-	-	-	-
Total direct transfers				72	396	142	306	38	485	1 937	0.1	1 545	1 354
Total tax expenditure				-	-	-	-	-	-	-	-	-	-
Total				72	396	142	306	38	485	1 937	0.1	1 545	1 354
Total, OECD (2018) report				-	-	142	72	38	43	-	-	-	-

Notes:

a. n.a.: not applicable, -: not available.

b. Where the subsidy is provided to more than one sector or fuel, its value in the country table may be somewhat different from the value reported in the OECD Inventory database due to disaggregation across sectors (see Annex I for further explanation). Values of electricity subsidies as reported in the country tables and the online database may also differ. Any difference has occurred because the non-fossil fuel component in electricity generation, as well as in imported electricity, has been subtracted from the electricity subsidy value for the purposes of the OECD database.

Source: Authors' compilations and calculations based on data collected for OECD (2020[1]) and previous estimates of fossil-fuel subsidies in the EaP countries published in OECD (2018[2]).

References

OECD (2020), "OECD-IEA Analysis of Fossil Fuels Support", webpage, http://www.oecd.org/fossil-fuels/publication/ (accessed on 20 May 2020). [1]

OECD (2018), *Inventory of Energy Subsidies in the EU's Eastern Partnership Countries*, Green Finance and Investment, OECD Publishing, Paris, https://doi.org/10.1787/9789264284319-en. [2]

Annex D. Belarus FFSs

Table A D.1. Fossil-fuel subsidies in Belarus, BYN million

Programme	Mechanism of support	Indicator	Fuel	2010	2011	2012	2013	2014	2015	2016	2017	2018	2019
Funding for construction (reconstruction) of energy infrastructure in residential areas	direct transfer	PSE	electricity, natural gas	354 000	-	575 785	1 292 344	1 151 319	-	134	137	101	106
Development of power grid and gas supply networks in rural areas	direct transfer	PSE	electricity, natural gas	n.a.	n.a.	n.a.	n.a.	n.a.	n.a.	-	39	28	37
Budget transfer to state enterprise "Minskenergo" to finance the reconstruction of heat networks	direct transfer	PSE	natural gas, fuel oil	n.a.	n.a.	n.a.	n.a.	n.a.	220 000	n.a.	n.a.	n.a.	n.a.
State support for development of the peat industry	direct transfer	PSE	peat	96 266	170 157	55 903	59 646	64 477	62 067	6	36	44	35
State spending on the modernisation of fixed assets of the energy system	direct transfer	PSE	electricity, natural gas, fuel oil, peat	811 281	n.a.	n.a.	n.a.	n.a.	n.a.	n.a.	n.a.	n.a.	n.a.
Budget transfers to compensate the costs of utility providers	direct transfer	CSE	electricity, natural gas, fuel oil, peat	-	-	-	-	-	-	-	-	-	-
Housing subsidies for low-income households	direct transfer	CSE	electricity, natural gas, fuel oil, peat	-	-	-	-	-	-	-	-	-	-
VAT exemption for utility tariffs for households	tax expenditure	CSE	electricity, natural gas, fuel oil, peat	507 000	626 000	1 007 000	1 335 000	2 038 000	-	n.a.	n.a.	n.a.	n.a.
Environmental tax relief for power plants providing electricity and heat for households	tax expenditure	CSE	electricity, natural gas, fuel oil, peat	-	-	-	-	-	-	-	-	-	-
Total direct transfers				**1 261 548**	**170 157**	**631 688**	**1 351 990**	**1 215 796**	**282 067**	**140**	**212**	**173**	**177**
Total tax expenditure				**507 000**	**626 000**	**1 007 000**	**1 335 000**	**2 038 000**	-	-	-	-	-
Total				1 768 548	796 157	1 638 688	2 686 990	3 253 796	282 067	140	212	173	177
Total, OECD (2018) report				3 111 000	6 264 000	13 491 000	13 856 000	17 493 000	-	-	-	-	-

Notes:

a. n.a.: not applicable, -: not available.

b. Where the subsidy is provided to more than one sector or fuel, its value in the country table may be somewhat different from the value reported in the OECD Inventory database due to disaggregation across sectors (see Annex I for further explanation). Values of electricity subsidies as reported in the country tables and the online database may also differ. Any difference has occurred because the non-fossil fuel component in electricity generation, as well as in imported electricity, has been subtracted from the electricity subsidy value for the purposes of the OECD database.

c. On 1 July 2016, the Belarusian Ruble was redenominated in a ratio 1:10 000. This explains the dramatic decline in subsidy values since 2016.

Source: Authors' compilations and calculations based on data collected for OECD (2020[1]) and previous estimates of fossil-fuel subsidies in the EaP countries published in OECD (2018[2]).

References

OECD (2020), "OECD-IEA Analysis of Fossil Fuels Support", webpage, http://www.oecd.org/fossil-fuels/publication/ (accessed on 20 May 2020).   [1]

OECD (2018), *Inventory of Energy Subsidies in the EU's Eastern Partnership Countries*, Green Finance and Investment, OECD Publishing, Paris, https://doi.org/10.1787/9789264284319-en.   [2]

Annex E. Georgia FFSs

Table A E.1. Fossil-fuel subsidies in Georgia, GEL million

Programme	Mechanism of support	Indicator	Fuel	2010	2011	2012	2013	2014	2015	2016	2017	2018	2019
Tax exemptions to oil- and gas-producing companies for certain operations	tax expenditure	PSE	natural gas, crude oil	7.4	6.1	6.9	6.9	7.1	8.8	9.1	9.5	9.5	10.4
Full cost compensation for the provision of free gas to households in the Kazbegi and Dusheti municipalities	direct transfer	CSE	natural gas	4.4	5.3	4.3	3.9	3.3	4.3	4.1	6.7	7.4	8.0
Utility subsidy for socially vulnerable households in Tbilisi municipality	direct transfer	CSE	electricity	n.a.	n.a.	6.4	44.2	45.1	47.0	25.6	7.3	7.3	8.3
Gas subsidy for households living on the border of Abkhazia and South Ossetia	direct transfer	CSE	natural gas	n.a.	n.a.	n.a.	n.a.	n.a.	n.a.	n.a.	2.0	2.4	2.6
Electricity subsidies for households in high mountainous areas	direct transfer	CSE	electricity	n.a.	n.a.	n.a.	n.a.	n.a.	n.a.	n.a.	6.6	9.3	9.8
Electricity subsidy for socially vulnerable consumers	direct transfer	CSE	electricity	n.a.	n.a.	n.a.	n.a.	n.a.	1.5	3.8	3.0	2.7	2.9
Electricity subsidy for families with four or more children	direct transfer	CSE	electricity	n.a.	n.a.	n.a.	n.a.	n.a.	n.a.	n.a.	n.a.	n.a.	0.1
Total direct transfers				4.4	5.3	10.7	48.1	48.4	52.8	33.5	25.6	29.2	31.6
Total tax expenditure				7.4	6.1	6.9	6.9	7.1	8.8	9.1	9.5	9.5	10.4
Total				11.8	11.4	17.5	55.0	55.5	61.6	42.6	35.1	38.7	42.0
Total, OECD (2018) report				219	368	390.4	365	428	-	-	-	-	-

Notes:

a. n.a.: not applicable, -: not available.

b. Where the subsidy is provided to more than one sector or fuel, its value in the country table may be somewhat different from the value reported in the OECD Inventory database due to disaggregation across sectors (see Annex I for further explanation). Values of electricity subsidies as reported in the country tables and the online database may also differ. Any difference has occurred because the non-fossil fuel component in electricity generation, as well as in imported electricity, has been subtracted from the electricity subsidy value for the purposes of the OECD database.

Source: Authors' compilations and calculations based on data collected for OECD (2020[1]) and previous estimates of fossil-fuel subsidies in the EaP countries published in OECD (2018[2]).

References

OECD (2020), "OECD-IEA Analysis of Fossil Fuels Support", webpage, http://www.oecd.org/fossil-fuels/publication/ (accessed on 20 May 2020). [1]

OECD (2018), *Inventory of Energy Subsidies in the EU's Eastern Partnership Countries*, Green Finance and Investment, OECD Publishing, Paris, https://doi.org/10.1787/9789264284319-en. [2]

Annex F. Moldova FFSs

Table A F.1. Fossil-fuel subsidies in Moldova, MDL million

Programme	Mechanism of support	Indicator	Fuel	2010	2011	2012	2013	2014	2015	2016	2017	2018	2019
Reduced VAT rates for natural gas consumed by households and public institutions	tax expenditure	CSE	natural gas	206.92	248.90	271.83	254.33	253.63	254.49	260.60	269.50	259.49	-
Reduced VAT rates for electricity consumed by households	tax expenditure	CSE	electricity	404.72	440.47	480.66	503.42	519.58	558.07	509.16	501.58	484.88	-
Reduced VAT rates for heating provided to households	tax expenditure	CSE	natural gas	191.91	234.31	240.08	217.19	217.98	234.52	260.58	253.20	278.01	-
Reduced VAT rates for LPG consumption	tax expenditure	CSE	LPG	73.31	92.57	118.58	95.58	99.25	118.70	73.38	82.98	80.86	-
Partial compensation for natural gas and electricity costs for households on the Transdnistria border	direct transfer	CSE	electricity, natural gas	17.80	24.31	22.59	24.86	25.57	22.06	21.63	30.61	24.97	-
Partial compensation of Chisinau households for energy resources costs	direct transfer	CSE	electricity, natural gas, coal	n.a	n.a	77.10	74.30	52.50	55.60	62.40	65.70	75.70	-
Public investment in natural gas pipelines and electricity grids	direct transfer	GSSE	electricity, natural gas	-	0.003	0.003	0.03	0.10	0.04	0.07	0.0002	-	-
Total direct transfers				17.80	24.31	99.69	99.19	78.17	77.70	84.10	96.31	100.67	-
Total tax expenditure				876.85	1 016.25	1 111.15	1 070.53	1 090.45	1 165.78	1 103.72	1 107.26	1 103.25	-
Total				894.65	1 040.56	1 210.84	1 169.72	1 168.62	1 243.47	1 187.82	1 203.57	1 203.91	-
Total, OECD (2018) report				-	1 717.21	2 183.65	2 144.97	2 621	971.56	-	-	-	-

Notes:

a. n.a.: not applicable, -: not available.

b. Where the subsidy is provided to more than one sector or fuel, its value in the country table may be somewhat different from the value reported in the OECD Inventory database due to disaggregation across sectors (see Annex I for further explanation). Values of electricity subsidies as reported in the country tables and the online database may also differ. Any difference has occurred because the non-fossil fuel component in electricity generation, as well as in imported electricity, has been subtracted from the electricity subsidy value for the purposes of the OECD database.

Source: Authors' compilations and calculations based on data collected for OECD (2020)[1] and previous estimates of fossil-fuel subsidies in the EaP countries published in OECD (2018)[2]).

References

OECD (2020), "OECD-IEA Analysis of Fossil Fuels Support", webpage, http://www.oecd.org/fossil-fuels/publication/ (accessed on 20 May 2020). [1]

OECD (2018), *Inventory of Energy Subsidies in the EU's Eastern Partnership Countries*, Green Finance and Investment, OECD Publishing, Paris, https://doi.org/10.1787/9789264284319-en. [2]

Annex G. Ukraine FFSs

Table A G.1. Fossil-fuel subsidies in Ukraine, UAH million

Programme	Mechanism of support	Indicator	Fuel	2010	2011	2012	2013	2014	2015	2016	2017	2018	2019
Restructuring of coal and peat industry	direct transfer	PSE	coal	1 059	1 597	1 078	1 178	355	206	107	244	n.a.	3 269
Decommissioning of unprofitable coal and peat mining enterprises	direct transfer	PSE	coal	n.a.	n.a.	n.a.	n.a.	n.a.	n.a.	n.a.	n.a.	281	128
Rescue measures at coal mining enterprises	direct transfer	PSE	coal	275	379	414	430	288	234	263	288	290	289
Prevention and elimination of emergencies at coal mines	direct transfer	PSE	coal	n.a.	1.1	n.a.	0.4	n.a.	n.a.	n.a.	10	82	n.a.
Liquidation of emergency at the main gas pipeline "Luhansk – Lysychansk – Rubezhnoye"	direct transfer	PSE	natural gas	n.a.	n.a.	n.a.	n.a.	n.a.	n.a.	n.a.	35	n.a.	n.a.
Liquidation of emergency at "Vuhlehirska" thermal power plant	direct transfer	PSE	electricity	n.a.	n.a.	n.a.	111	n.a.	n.a.	n.a.	n.a.	n.a.	n.a.
Partial compensation of production costs of finished marketable coal	direct transfer	PSE	coal	5 807	6 710	10 172	13 302	8 705	1 212	1 373	2 122	1 072	n.a.
Improvement of safety measures at coal mining enterprises	direct transfer	PSE	coal	70	134	260	197	3	n.a.	n.a.	99	n.a.	n.a.
Construction and technical re-equipment of coal and peat mining enterprises	direct transfer	PSE	coal	337	1 719	1 293	343	54	n.a.	n.a.	n.a.	n.a.	n.a.
Replenishment of current capital or increase of the statutory funds of coal mines to settle wage arrears	direct transfer	PSE	coal	n.a.	n.a.	n.a.	n.a.	n.a.	200	500	n.a.	n.a.	n.a.
Repayment for electricity arrears of state-owned coal-mining enterprises	direct transfer	PSE	coal	140	n.a.	n.a.	n.a.	n.a.	n.a.	n.a.	n.a.	n.a.	445
State support for the construction of mine No. 10 "Novovolynska"	direct transfer	PSE	coal	n.a.	n.a.	n.a.	n.a.	n.a.	146	50	70	35	62

Programme	Mechanism of support	Indicator	Fuel	2010	2011	2012	2013	2014	2015	2016	2017	2018	2019
Measures to support domestic production of coal and reform of the coal sector	direct transfer	PSE	coal	n.a.	n.a.	n.a.	n.a.	n.a.	n.a.	n.a.	n.a.	1 671	n.a.
State support for the PJSC "Mahistralni Gazoprovody Ukrainy" (Main Gas Pipelines of Ukraine)	direct transfer	PSE	natural gas	n.a.	n.a.	n.a.	n.a.	n.a.	n.a.	n.a.	0.1	20	n.a.
Compensation to NJSC "Naftogaz of Ukraine" for the difference between the purchase prices of imported natural gas and its sale for heat production for households	direct transfer	CSE	natural gas	3 424	n.a.	3 900	n.a.	n.a.	n.a.	n.a.	n.a.	n.a.	n.a.
Budget transfer to Smilakomunteploenergo to prevent an emergency in the Town of Smila due to the financial inability of the enterprise to pay for natural gas	direct transfer	CSE	natural gas	n.a.	n.a.	n.a.	n.a.	n.a.	n.a.	n.a.	n.a.	n.a.	15
Transfer (subvention) from the state budget to local budgets to compensate for the difference between actual costs of utilities and tariffs set	direct transfer	CSE	natural gas, electricity, coal, fuel oil	n.a.	2 857	14 443	2 052	12 423	4 685	n.a.	1 798	978	n.a.
Transfer (subvention) from the state budget to local budgets for the provision of benefits and housing subsidies for utility payment to low-income households[c]	direct transfer	CSE	natural gas, electricity, coal, fuel oil	5 131	6 069	6 718	6 046	6 173	17 995	44 120	69 740	69 977	21 561
Transfer (subvention) from the state budget to local budgets for the provision of benefits and housing subsidies for purchasing of solid and liquid household furnace fuel and LPG for low-income households	direct transfer	CSE	LPG, fuel oil, coal	496	557	738	733	715	1 121	2 280	2 633	2 694	1 820
Direct payments of benefits and housing subsidies to households to partially cover utility, solid and liquid furnace fuel and LPG costs[d]	direct transfer	CSE	natural gas, electricity, coal, fuel oil	n.a.	n.a.	n.a.	n.a.	n.a.	n.a.	n.a.	n.a.	n.a.	23 267
Corporate income tax deduction for expenditure of energy enterprises planned within investment programmes	tax expenditure	PSE	electricity, oil, natural gas	n.a.	263	975	761	957	n.a.	n.a.	n.a.	n.a.	n.a.
Corporate income tax credit for the amount of excise tax levied on heavy distillates (gasoil) used in transport vehicles	tax expenditure	PSE	diesel	n.a.	n.a.	n.a.	n.a.	n.a.	n.a.	n.a.	n.a.	735	639

Programme	Mechanism of support	Indicator	Fuel	2010	2011	2012	2013	2014	2015	2016	2017	2018	2019
Corporate income tax deduction for costs associated with exploration and organisation of oil and gas fields	tax expenditure	PSE	oil, natural gas		23		n.a.	n.a.	n.a.	n.a.	n.a.	n.a.	n.a.
Temporary VAT relief for operations related to natural gas supply imported into the customs territory of Ukraine by the NJSK "Naftogaz of Ukraine"	tax expenditure	PSE	natural gas	n.a.	575	1 464	n.a.	n.a.	n.a.	n.a.	n.a.	n.a.	n.a.
Temporary VAT relief for supply of coal and/or products of its enrichment on the customs territory of Ukraine	tax expenditure	PSE	coal, lignite, peat, coke	n.a.	n.a.	n.a.	n.a.	n.a.	n.a.	2 116	2 609	3 042	3 608
Excise tax relief for operations related to the sale of LPG at specialised auctions for the needs of households	tax expenditure	CSE	LPG	n.a.	13	69	78	78	14	14	109	65	70
Total direct transfers				16 739	20 023	39 017	24 393	28 716	25 799	48 693	77 040	77 101	50 856
Total tax expenditure				-	874	2 507	839	1 036	14	2 130	2 717	3 841	4 317
Total				16 739	20 897	41 524	25 232	29 752	25 813	822	79 757	80 942	55 173
Total, OECD (2018) report						124 870	114 933	202 829	153 489				

Notes:

a. n.a.: not applicable, -: not available.

b. Where the subsidy is provided to more than one sector or fuel, its value in the country table may be somewhat different from the value reported in the OECD Inventory database due to disaggregation across sectors (see Annex I for further explanation). Values of electricity subsidies as reported in the country tables and the online database may also differ. Any difference has occurred because the non-fossil fuel component in electricity generation, as well as in imported electricity, has been subtracted from the electricity subsidy value for the purposes of the OECD database.

c. Benefits and housing subsidies cover all utility payments including electricity, natural gas, heat, water supply and sewerage services, maintenance of the building, waste management. At the time of drafting this report, detailed data for disaggregation of this measure between energy and non-energy consumption were unavailable. However, energy consumption clearly accounts for the largest share of household utility bills. These values are further adjusted in the OECD Inventory database based on IEA (2020[1]) energy balances data.

d. Idem.

Source: Authors' compilations and calculations based on data collected for OECD (2020[2]) and previous estimates of fossil-fuel subsidies in the EaP countries published in OECD (2018[4]).

References

IEA (2020), "Data and statistics", *Energy Balances Statistics*, (database), https://www.iea.org/data-and-statistics/data-tables?country=WORLD (accessed on 14 January 2021). [1]

OECD (2020), "OECD-IEA Analysis of Fossil Fuels Support", webpage, http://www.oecd.org/fossil-fuels/publication/ (accessed on 20 May 2020). [2]

OECD (2018), *Inventory of Energy Subsidies in the EU's Eastern Partnership Countries*, Green Finance and Investment, OECD Publishing, Paris, https://doi.org/10.1787/9789264284319-en. [3]

Annex H. Covid-related measures

Table A H.1. Main government COVID-19 related support measures in the energy sector in EaP countries

	Total COVID-related public support	Specific energy-related support measures	Estimated amount for energy-related measures	Source
Armenia	AMD 150 billion (USD 305 million)	Reimbursement of electricity and natural gas utility bills of eligible consumers. A total of 728 000 household users of electricity and 503 000 households using gas benefited from this measure in February 2020. The support is transferred directly from the state budget to the utilities selling natural gas and electricity on the basis of clearly identified consumers who need help.	AMD 4.3 billion (USD 9 million)	https://armeniasputnik.am/armenia/20200430/22901932/petrvari-komunalnern-el-kpoxhatucven-pashinyany-haytnec-ovqer-kstanan-ajakc:utyuny.html
Azerbaijan	AZN 2.6 billion (USD 1.5 billion)	Government support programme "100 kWh of preferential light limit for the population in April-May 2020".	AZN 10 million (USD 5.9 million)	https://cabmin.gov.az/az/document/4367/
Belarus	BYN 5 to 6 billion (USD 2 to 2.5 billion)	Partial reimbursement (up to 20%) for households was introduced for costs incurred for improving the power supply of the housing stock (heating, hot water supply and cooking), including expenses for the purchase of equipment to incentivise increased electricity use for these services. The individual compensation cannot be higher than 40 basic units (1 basic unit = BYN 27, about USD 11, or about USD 495 in total). An estimated 15 000 consumers will benefit from this measure. The cost of this direct subsidy will be covered by local budgets.

The Belarusian government has not yet determined the exact timeframe for transition to a full cost recovery for heat and gas supply services for households. | BYN 15.2 million (USD 6.2 million) | Decree of the President of the Republic of Belarus No 127 of 14 April 2020 on Recovery of Costs Related to the Power Supply of the Existing Housing Stock |
| **Georgia** | GEL 3.5 billion (USD 1.1 billion) | Reimbursement of household utility bills for the three months of March – May 2020. Only households that did not consume more than 200 kWh of electricity and/or 200 m³ of natural gas received the subsidy. In monetary terms, in the case of electricity, JSC "Telasi" clients received up to GEL 37 per month, while the subsidy for JSC "ENERGO-PRO" clients was GEL 36 per month. "Tbilisi Energy' natural gas clients could receive a subsidy only if their bill was not higher than GEL 92. "SOCAR" users received a subsidy of GEL 114. More than 1.2 million electricity customers and more than 670 000 natural gas customers participated in the subsidy scheme.

All consumers eligible for this state support could decline it. In these three months, more than 9 600 consumers declined to receive the subsidy as a sign of solidarity. In March 2020, 3 534 consumers declined to join the scheme; in April, more than 4 600 consumers declined. | GEL 150 million (USD 49 million) | https://bit.ly/31bOSr1, https://bit.ly/2YnIOuO, https://bit.ly/2Yrd33a, https://bit.ly/3es8J9g, https://bit.ly/3hRrmn83 |

	Total COVID-related public support	Specific energy-related support measures	Estimated amount for energy-related measures	Source
Moldova	LEU 2.5 billion (USD 150 million)	No specific direct support scheme identified. However, a regulation banning the disconnection of customers in case of late payment for communal services, including for electricity and heat, was introduced.		Government of Moldova
Ukraine	UAH 65 billion (USD 2.4 billion)	A Stabilisation Fund was established within the general fund of the state budget to cover the quarantine period. Thirty days after the end of the quarantine, the fund is expected to be closed down. As of 13 April 2020, the total value of the fund was UAH 64.7 billion (USD 2.4 billion). No specific measures for the energy sector were identified as part of the Stabilisation Fund. However, analysis of the planned budget spending before the crisis (January 2020) and after budget amendments were approved in April 2020 shows the government revised budget spending in the energy sector, too. Spending on a couple of state support programmes in the coal sector was reduced, but expenditure on the restructuring of the coal sector nearly doubled. This resulted in an increase of subsidies to the coal sector by UAH 837 million (USD 30 million).	UAH 837 million (USD 31 million)	Parliament of Ukraine (2019), Law of Ukraine on 2020 State Budget No. 294-IX of 14 November 2019 (with Amendments), https://zakon.rada.gov.ua/laws/show/294-20#Text

Source: Total public support based on information provided in OECD (2020)[11].

References

OECD (2020), "COVID-19 crisis response in Eastern Partner countries", *OECD Policy Responses to Coronavirus (COVID-19)*, 13 October, OECD, Paris, http://www.oecd.org/coronavirus/policy-responses/covid-19-crisis-response-in-eu-eastern-partner-countries-7759afa3/#section-d1e1382. [1]

Annex I. OECD Fossil-Fuel support database

Breaking down fossil-fuel support data to economic sector beneficiaries in the OECD Inventory Database

When first launched, the OECD Inventory of Support Measures for Fossil Fuels was organised following the OECD's Producer Support Estimate[1] – Consumer Support Estimate[2] (PSE-CSE) framework. Under this framework, measures providing benefits to fossil-fuel producers are classified under PSE, while those that provide benefits to individual fossil-fuel consumers fall under CSE. A third category, the General Services Support Estimate[3] (GSSE), is assigned to measures that do not increase production or consumption of fossil fuels at present but may do so in the future.

The PSE-CSE classification framework is broad enough and does not allow further disaggregation of beneficiaries by economic sector. It can isolate which measures benefit the upstream or midstream fossil-fuel sectors. However, it is difficult to isolate and pinpoint in greater detail the final end-user economic sectors (e.g. industrial, transport, residential, commercial, agriculture, fisheries, etc.) targeted by fossil-fuel measures. Identifying and quantifying the benefit received by each economic sector in fossil-fuel support is key to evaluate the distributional impacts of proposed fossil-fuel reforms. It is also needed to evaluate whether a targeted support programme is efficient in reaching its intended beneficiaries.

The OECD recently further improved disaggregation of beneficiaries by economic sectors to better identify the end-user economic sectors that benefit from government fossil-fuel support. To that end, it introduced sector tagging mechanisms for each support measure in the database.

Sector tagging mechanics for fossil-fuel support measures

For each measure in the Inventory, two types of information are provided: i) fiscal information on the budgetary transfers or tax expenditure (monetary value); and ii) textual metadata with contents on a measure's beneficiaries, eligibility criteria, historical background and any relevant budgetary data, procurement and processing information.

Information on the textual metadata is used to identify which economic sector benefits from each measure. In tagging each measure, the economic activity nomenclature follows the classification used in the IEA *World Energy Balances* flows.[4] Measures can receive a single (in case only one economic sector gets the benefits) or multiple sector tags. In case of a single sector tag, the attribution of values is straightforward and the whole value of the measure gets assigned to the single sector. However, there are cases where a measure is designed to benefit multiple sectors (e.g. preferential tax rates for natural gas targeting both residential and commercial sectors). In this case, allocations to each sector are based on calculated proportions from the reported energy consumption figures in the IEA *World Energy Balances*.

Finally, after the sector tagging exercise, the results are aggregated and mapped according to the broad sectoral categories in Table A I.1.

Table A I.1. Selected tags for sectoral disaggregation of fossil-fuel support measures

Broad sector	Remarks and included sectors (IEA short names)
Fossil-fuel production	This category comprises measures that benefit the upstream and midstream segment of fossil-fuel production. It includes measures targeted towards the exploration, production, trade (import or export), transportation or storage of fossil fuels. Each type of measure is given a certain code in the database, such as: INDPROD, IMPORTS, EXPORTS, STOCKCHA or TES (Total energy supply) (if no detail available).
Electricity generation	This category represents measures that provide support to fossil fuels used as inputs in power generation. Only input fuels fall under this category. It does not include support for consumption of electricity by end-use consumers. Each type of measure is given a certain code in the database, such as: MAINELEC, AUTOELEC, MAINCHP, AUTOCHP, MAINHEAT, AUTOHEAT.
Transport	Measures in this category cover fuels used in the following transport activities: road vehicles, agricultural and industrial highway use, aircraft for domestic aviation, rail traffic (including urban or suburban transport systems), energy used for pipelines transporting fossil fuels, domestic maritime navigation (i.e. port of departure and arrival of the same country), and all transport not specified elsewhere. Each type of measure is given a certain code in the database, such as: DOMESAIR, ROAD, RAIL, PIPELINE, DOMESNAV, TRNONSPE.
Residential	Measures classified under the residential sector include consumption by households (including households with employed persons), with fuels used for transport.
Other sectors	Other sectors include measures that support use of fossil fuels in energy transformation other than electricity and heat generation, industry and manufacturing, commercial and public services, agriculture, forestry and fisheries and non-energy use. Each type of measure is given a certain code in the database, such as: THEAT, TBOILER, TELE, TBLASTFUR, TGASWKS, TCOKEOVS, TPATFUEL, TBKB, TREFINER, TPETCHEM, LIQUEFAC, TNONSPEC, OWNUSE, EMINES, EOILGASEX, EBLASTFUR, EGASWKS, EBIOGAS, ECOKEOVS, EPATFUEL, EBKB, EREFINER, ECOALLIQ, ELNG, EGTL, EPOWERPLT, EPUMPST, ENUC, ECHARCOAL, ENONSPEC, TRANSFER. IRONSTL, CHEMICAL, NONMET, PAPERPRO, NONFERR, TEXTILES, MINING, TRANSEQ, MACHINE, FOODPRO, PAPERPRO, WOODPRO, CONSTRUC, INONSPEC. RESIDENT, AGRICULT, FISHING, COMMPUB, ONONSPEC, NONENUSE.

Source: Adapted from IEA (IEA, 2020[1]) and IEA *World Energy Statistics and Balances* (database).

The routines were implemented using Stata to automate the allocation of each measure. At the end of the tagging exercise, each measure is classified according to three dimensions: a) fuel(s) benefited; b) PSE-CSE indicator; and c) sector beneficiaries. For the sectoral aggregates, allocation is done in dual dimensions, with more than 100 fuel-sector combinations. This made the calculation computationally-intensive, with the dual dimension structure requiring $O(n^2)$ polynomial time complexity.

The disaggregation is conducted when certain subsidy schemes benefit more than one economic sector or fuel. Therefore, the values of such subsidy measures in the country tables of this report may differ from values published in the OECD Inventory online database. In addition, the values of electricity subsidies reported in the country tables and in the online database may also differ. This may occur because the non-fossil-fuel component in electricity generation has been subtracted from the electricity subsidy value for the purposes of the OECD database.

References

IEA (2020), "Data and statistics", *Energy Balances Statistics*, (database), https://www.iea.org/data-and-statistics/data-tables?country=WORLD (accessed on 14 January 2021). [1]

Notes

[1] The Producer Support Estimate (PSE) indicator measures the annual value of transfers from consumers and taxpayers to producers of fossil fuels.

[2] Consumer Support Estimate (CSE) reflects the value of transfers to consumers of fossil fuels regardless of their nature, objectives or impacts on consumption.

[3] General Support Services Estimates (GSSE) represents the value of transfers arising from policy measures that create enabling conditions for the fossil-fuel sector. These conditions are created through the development of private or public services, institutions and infrastructure regardless of their objectives and impact on fossil-fuel production and/or consumption. GSSE includes policies where fossil fuels are the main beneficiaries but does not include any payments to individual producers. GSSE transfers do not directly alter producer receipts or costs, or consumption expenditure, although they may affect production or consumption of fossil fuels in the long term.

[4] For more information see: http://wds.iea.org/wds/pdf/WORLDBAL_Documentation.pdf.

www.ingramcontent.com/pod-product-compliance
Lightning Source LLC
Chambersburg PA
CBHW081512200326
41518CB00015B/2472